NARRATIVE PICTURES

I. THE BLIND GIRL

Sir John E. Millais

The City of Birmingham Art Gallery

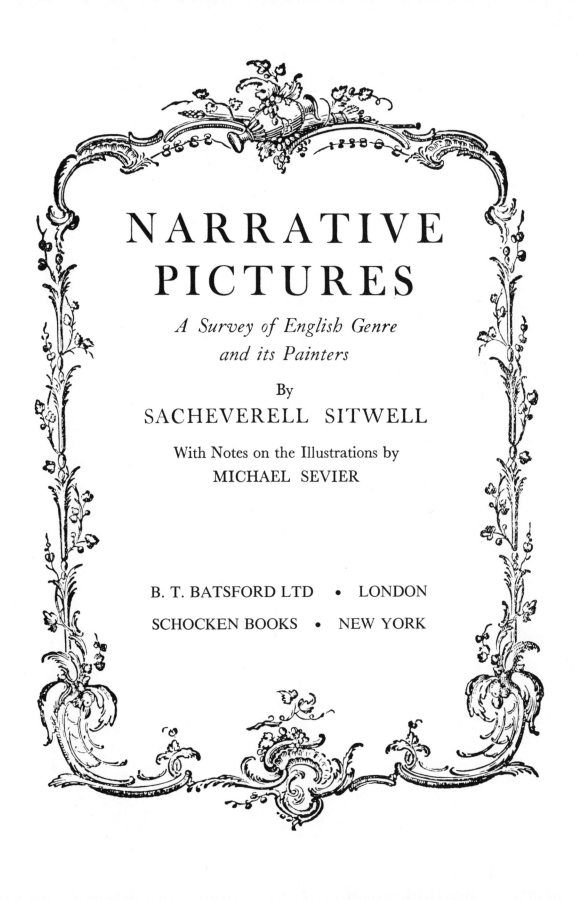

NARRATIVE PICTURES

A Survey of English Genre
and its Painters

By

SACHEVERELL SITWELL

With Notes on the Illustrations by
MICHAEL SEVIER

B. T. BATSFORD LTD • LONDON

SCHOCKEN BOOKS • NEW YORK

This volume is a faithful reproduction of the first printing, Batsford, 1936,
with the exception that the colour plates have been reproduced in monochrome.

First published in this format in 1969 by
B. T. Batsford Ltd
4 Fitzhardinge Street, London W 1

and

Schocken Books Inc.
67 Park Avenue, New York, N.Y. 10016

Library of Congress Catalog Card No. 69–19623

Manufactured in the United States of America

CONTENTS

PREFACE

IN writing this book, the object of which is to establish a school or body of English Narrative Painting, innumerable books have had to be consulted. It would be superfluous, and more certainly redundant, to set down all their names. The author can only state his repeated obligations to all concerned. All owners of the pictures illustrated must be thanked, individually and collectively, for their kind services in allowing reproductions to be made; a special note of thanks being due, more particularly, to Henry Reitlinger, Esq., Sir Edward Marsh, Henry Harris, Esq., Brinsley Ford, Esq., Guy Repton, Esq., Oliver Brown, Esq., and C. L. Phillips, Esq., of the Leicester Galleries, Miss L. Simpson, of the Knoedler Galleries, and Sir Robert Witt, for the repeated help and advice of his library staff. Finally, the author would like to express his gratitude to Mr. Michael Sevier, who has worked so tirelessly upon the notes and the illustrations, and to Mr. Charles Fry who, once again, has been the inspirer and the source of energy behind this task.

SACHEVERELL SITWELL.

October, 1937.

NARRATIVE PICTURES

CHAPTER I

INTRODUCTION

IT has been said too often of British painting that its inspiration lies always in literature. As painters, our artists are no better than illustrators of poetry or fiction. This is the charge; and certainly it is circumstantial in many of its details. If Gainsborough and Constable and Turner are in contradiction to this, Hogarth, Zoffany, the Pre-Raphaelites, Rowlandson, Cruikshank are the proving of it. Theirs is the indisputable literary background. It has seemed better, therefore, not to deny these allegations but to collect together as much evidence as possible in support of them. And, in the course of this process, some clear presentment may emerge of what is, beyond any doubt, our native predilection in painting.

It would be better, at once, to attempt the definition of our subject. Perhaps the most easy explanation would be to term it the painting of anecdote. It is the chosen moment in some related incident, and looking more closely into its details we must see hints or suggestions of the before and after of the story. The Last Day in the Old Home (115) is a perfect example of this genre of painting. So is Frith's Derby Day (119); while the method can be extended into a whole series of pictures until we get to Marriage à la Mode or A Rake's Progress. By now, and merely through the aid of such well-known names, the most recognizable principles of this form of painting should be established. The pursuit of specimens will take us over much familiar ground, so hackneyed as to be ready for rediscovery; but, also, it is likely to reveal a good many excellent and unknown things to some of which, if the word is at all applicable in British painting, the term of lesser or minor masterpiece must surely be accorded, where paintings so characteristic and with such forgotten qualities are concerned.

Already, enough has been said to proclaim William Hogarth as the initiator and leader of the school. Hogarth was a person who prophesied, in the eighteenth century, much of the complacency of the Victorian time. He is the only—almost the only—painter to give us that century shorn of its elegancies. It has always been said that we should be grateful to him for this; but there are moods in which Hogarth is too strongly the mid-Victorian in his insistence on necessary and commonplace ugliness. This relates him to something which is indelible in our national character. It is even possible, in Hogarth, to be reminded of the late Victorian novels of Mr. H. G. Wells. If he is in this relationship to Wells, Hogarth is closer still to Dickens. But these intangible ties of blood begin to give us his stature. Hogarth is a great man, a great painter; but, like Dickens, or H. G. Wells, or Bernard Shaw, he is not an artist, that is to say he is lacking in all poetry or sense of beauty. He denies it and does not care for it; and in a land where literature is the tradition, and poetry is the half and the supreme fame of that, the absence of any poetry is a severe condemnation. Those who are deficient in it, whatever their qualities may be of wit or satire, are brought perilously near to the brim of journalism. The salvation of Hogarth from this danger is that he was more of a dramatist than a writer. His pictures are scenes from plays: it is the spoken literature of the drama that is his closest parallel. We shall see that Hogarth, himself, spoke of his own paintings as 'pictur'd morals.' The insistence, in his phrase, is upon the morals being interpreted in a new and unexpected medium. His theory is not so much an enlargement of the possibilities in painting as the discovery of another vehicle by which to point the moral and adorn the tale.

But Hogarth must be studied still further, for his essential importance has been recognized by every generation of English painter. He was the one painter proclaimed by Rossetti, and by the Pre-Raphaelites who spoke in chorus after him. He was singled out by them from a whole century of sin. Neither, in more recent times, has he been neglected. Orpen's diploma picture, The Rehearsal of Hamlet, is nothing less than a direct tribute to Hogarth. Living painters, Sickert and Augustus John, have also shown their homage to him. It is to be accepted, then, that Hogarth is a painter who is indispensable from any consideration of the English achievement in painting. This is, quite simply, because he is the primitive of the whole school. It is a curious thought, though, to consider the companions who chose him out for company. Hogarth, who we may think it certain would have been on the side of Dickens in his satirical comments upon the Pre-Raphaelites brethren, could not have found the aestheticism of Rossetti to his taste. The bedfellows sought in aesthetic enthusiasm could not have their oddity more pungently exemplified than in this curious conjunction.

The reason for it, of course, lies in Hogarth's fidelity of detail. This question of detail, as we shall discover later on when the painters of that school are called upon for examples, became not a means but an end.

2

2. NOON

William Hogarth

The Earl of Ancaster

3. THE DISTRESSED POET

William Hogarth   *The City of Birmingham Art Gallery*

4. THE GATE OF CALAIS

William Hogarth   *The National Gallery*

Detail for detail's sake is to be found in every picture of those few years when the combined influences of Ruskin and Rossetti produced some of the supreme curiosities in minor painting. That was in the 'fifties of last century; The Blind Girl (1) and The Hireling Shepherd (10) being two of the pictures to which we refer. These are as full of anecdotal detail as any painting by Hogarth. In the case of Hogarth, so trivial a thing as the 'thief' burning in the candle-flame becomes a symbol and a warning. Nothing is there without an excuse. If the scene depicts the interior of a room, every painting upon the walls, and the walls may be covered with them, will be a carefully composed satire or commentary upon the action of the persons concerned. This is the extreme of painstaking ingenuity; but it is not, and cannot be, the highest art. When we consider their positive excellence, a set of engravings like Cruikshank's The Bottle will become, for this reason, nearly as important as A Rake's Progress or Marriage à la Mode. This is because, in both cases, they are great illustrations and not great paintings. Cruikshank and Rowlandson, at their best, owing to the pedestrian terms on which Hogarth competed, are not inferior to the master from whom they derived. Hogarth, then, is a person to whom the appellation of a great painter can but seldom be applied. It is only true of him in exceptional instances. There are cases, though, in which he will surprise every considered opinion of him. Such are his splendid scene from The Indian Emperor, in Holland House, which is the finest of his Conversation Pieces; the scene from The Beggar's Opera; or Lord George Graham in his cabin; or the inimitable Taste in High Life. And with Hogarth, perhaps more than in the case of other painters, the picture when you see it will be different from your previous conception of it. This is because his pictures are known to us, in the first place, by the engravings that he made of them. The Calais Gate (4) is far larger and more important than might have been guessed; while A Rake's Progress may rather disappoint those who visit the Soane Museum by the smallness of its dimensions. The eight subjects of which it is composed are but little bigger than the engravings that are so familiar. 'Are these really the originals?' we might be tempted to ask, until a consideration of their minute and subdued excellencies begins to prevail over the first disillusionment.

Two factors, it would seem to us, must never be forgotten in Hogarth's character. In the first place, he was a real and true Cockney. It is difficult to find the country in any picture by his hand. In the second place, his sturdy and independent personality is to be explained in part because of his small stature. According to Vertue, his contemporary, Mr. Hogarth was under five feet high. This brings him very near to being a dwarf, for the limits of normal stature may be set, according to some authorities, between six feet six and four feet eleven. If you are the former you must be included among the giants; if the latter you are among the dwarfs. Hogarth, then, missed this by an inch or less. He had something of the proverbial obstinacy of the very small. Nothing was more strong in him than his conviction that he was in the right and that foreigners were in the wrong. Those who did not agree with him were condemned out of their own mouths. Thus Italian music, Italian architecture, Italian painting were always under his censure and are to be seen ridiculed at every turn in his pictures. Yet Hogarth was a person who had never been further abroad than a day, ending in an unfortunate incident, at Calais. He was, therefore, in no position to satirize French or Italian taste for he was altogether lacking in first-hand knowledge of it. In this, the Cockney side of his nature asserted itself. He was confident and quick-witted, and quite sure that the present was better than the past, even with the horrors of Gin Lane included. It was the extraordinary vitality of Hogarth and the wonders of his dramatic invention that made him the father of our painting.

In lifelong achievement Hogarth has never had an equal. He was not diverted, like Turner, into perilous experiments. He did not, as in the case of Gainsborough, who gave up landscape for portraiture, sacrifice his talent in order to achieve an easier success. He did not, like Millais, one of our greatest painters, collapse inexplicably and with a completeness that even a purely mercenary interest is unable to make credible or excuse. The original talents of Hogarth lasted him his lifetime and were undimmed until the end. It is to be argued that there were painters with an easier and more facile gift than his. George Morland, if his moral fibre had been stronger, could have achieved great things, but it was the very lack of this, perhaps, that gave him his effortless grace. So little painstaking, though, was George Morland that, for our purposes, it is next to impossible to make use of him. So airy and unsubstantial are his subjects, even when they deal with the barn or the farmyard, that they illustrate nothing. All that can be said of them is expressed in their own fluent and sentimental ease. A deadly seriousness, even in comical subjects, is essential to the painter of literary derivation. This is to be found, at first hand, in Zoffany, all of whose Conversation Pieces may be said to be illustrations of domestic or dramatic action. And, from Zoffany, the gulf is not so wide or deep as might be imagined that separates him from Madox Brown, or even from Augustus Egg. When differences in period are allowed for, the approach, in Zoffany's Tribuna of the Uffizi, is not so far different from the processes that were behind the imagination of Madox Brown in Work (11), his

4

5. THE LAPIDARIES

John Zoffany

6.   CONCERT OF WANDERING MINSTRELS

John Zoffany

Parma Gallery

diploma picture. In both pictures every conceivable thing had to be included; and, granted the powers of both painters, which were very considerable, Work and the Tribuna are not so far removed from each other in achievement. Their objects were not dissimilar and the finished results are of a comparable aesthetic value. It could be possible, too, to compare The Lapidaries by Zoffany (5) with the better-known Last of England by Madox Brown (111). In this instance Madox Brown, perhaps, would be judged the more successful, because of the added weight of the sentiment which inspired his painting. For it is a picture of a sentiment; while The Lapidaries has no sentiment whatever and not even a moral can be attached to it. Zoffany preferred dramatic action to sentiment. There is never sentiment in Hogarth. The appearance of this nervous weakness, coming in the middle years of the Victorian epoch, is a sign that the last days of this kind of painting are at hand.

Between Zoffany and Madox Brown there is, nevertheless, a distance which is immense, and its foreground is occupied by many utterly dissimilar things. Paintings and drawings by Fuseli, the entire creation of Cruikshank, the romanticism of Wilkie or Bonington, these are some of the things filling that void. For its duration was for nearly a century, and there must be many inevitable changes during the lives of three generations of men. After the death of Zoffany in the early years of the nineteenth century the most considerable figure to emerge is that of Fuseli. He had been born in 1741, and was therefore seventy years of age in 1810, when Zoffany died. At the same time his best works, which must belong to the years 1780 to 1800, belong, in spirit, to a generation later than that of Zoffany. He is the painter of the sham Gothick and of the Tales of Terror. And, in a curious way, he forestalls the literature and the music of a later generation. *Melmoth the Wanderer*, the work of Maturin, the Dublin clergyman, is implicit in the paintings of Fuseli. This novel, in the eighteen-twenties, was to have profound effect, not only in England but abroad. The young Balzac fell completely under its spell; *Melmoth the Wanderer* and the poems of Ossian, together, were the text-books of one phase of the Romantic Movement. If Fuseli is reflected in the novels of Maturin his shadow is to be found also in the operas of Marschner. *The Vampire*, as an opera, might be the direct inspiration of Fuseli. But both *Melmoth the Wanderer* and *The Vampire* are some fifty years later in date than the most characteristic of Fuseli's paintings. The Nightmare, which is reproduced in this volume (84), is one of the more famous of the pictures in question. It was painted in 1782. From our contemporary point of view, though, there is more that is interesting in the drawings of Fuseli. He

5

had too nearly the equipment of a writer to make a first-rate painter. His large pictures are nearly always a disappointment, but this is not so with his drawings. And these vary astonishingly in style. Many of them are weak and distorted Michelangelos. But, also, Fuseli had a great influence over William Blake, and there are many Fuselis which are strongly reminiscent of Blake; while other drawings, one or two of which are illustrated in this context, could be compared to Aubrey Beardsley at his best. The influence, here, seems to come from a curious Edinburgh artist, John Brown, a pupil of Alexander Runciman, another forgotten painter, whose chief work, a series of frescoes, at Penicuik, from subjects of Ossian, was unfortunately destroyed by fire. It is, therefore, next to impossible to judge of Runciman; while Brown, who seems to have died early of consumption, like Beardsley, is only preserved by a very few drawings which are nearly indistinguishable from those by Fuseli. Both artists travelled together in Italy; and that phase of Fuseli which we most admire is Fuseli working in the style and under the influence of John Brown.

Nothing could be more different than Fuseli from Hogarth: one has the poetic drama, and the other, the drama of comedy for his background. Fuseli, being a Swiss German from Zürich, had German Romanticism in his blood in its most sanguine and morbid forms. It must also be remembered that Fuseli was a devotee of Shakespeare. The reading of Shakespeare was as strong an influence in him as it was in Berlioz, who also belongs to this same movement in art. Berlioz is the case of a musician with a literary background. His early works, *King Lear*, *Les Francs-Juges*, even the *Symphonie Fantastique*, have Fuseli and Maturin and Marschner in them, even if these works were quite unknown to their author. Weber, at least, as a German Romantic, had a great influence over Berlioz, so that some of the influences that worked on Berlioz were at work on Fuseli. Both men, as we have said, are part of the same movement in art. It was a movement exclusively literary in its inspiration, and even when the forms that it produced were music or painting and not poetic dramas they are the offshoots of literature and are to be judged by some of its standards. This first flood of the Romantic Movement, in its ghost stories, in the *Castle of Otranto* or *Melmoth the Wanderer*, in its toy castles, in its paintings by Fuseli or Delacroix, in its music of Weber, or Marschner, or Berlioz, can all be ascribed to the processes of reading. It is the reading of poems and the reading of plays that inspired it.

A major part of the energies of Fuseli were devoted to Boydell's Shakespeare Gallery and to his own Milton Gallery. This latter project occupied him for several years and comprised, in the end, no fewer than fifty paintings. Both enterprises could be characterized as a waste of time; but Boydell's Shakespeare Gallery serves, at least, as an introduction to the works of the Rev. Matthew William Peters, an unequal painter who is, at moments, one of the best colourists of the English school. His paintings from the *Merry Wives of Windsor* are quite enchanting; but this odd personage, who combined the painting of *galanteries* with the post of chaplain to the Prince Regent, is something of a disappointment. None the less, he illustrates some of the tendencies of the late eighteenth century. And, in front of him, except for William Etty, there stretches a vista of unending seriousness. Etty, unfortunately for our purposes, is to be characterized as a painter of mythology, so that it is impossible to include even his delightful Youth at the Prow and Pleasure at the Helm among our illustrations. This is a definite and decided loss, for Etty is a delicate and sensual antidote to be taken just before the pulpit thunderings and denunciations of Ruskin.

It is pleasant also, before it is too late, to look at George Cruikshank, who has survived into the full tide of Victorian seriousness. We find him, at well over sixty years of age, working hard at oil painting and producing The Runaway Knock (8), or The Disturber Detected (97), two paintings which, if not very important, deserve at least to be restored from the neglect into which they have fallen. It has been a most pleasant task to illustrate this work with four or five forgotten paintings by one of the very greatest of English artists. Cruikshank is, and must always be, immortal, for he is the delineator of London life from the days of the Regency down till the Crystal Palace and the Great Exhibition. It is curious also, and this point must be considered at greater length later on in this book, that the few oil paintings by Cruikshank were done at a late date in his life but are really pictures of the world as he knew it in his youth. This conscious archaism, when dealing with the affairs or scenes of one's own life, is a rare thing not often to be found. Like those poems in which Swinburne purposely parodied himself they show the immense pains that are necessary to the building up of a personality, and that it is a conscious effort on the part of the creator.

And now, in the generation following upon Cruikshank, the full tide of momentary realism in painting, the semi-truths that are all that minute and painstaking detail can prove, gathers and accumulates and breaks its bonds. This phenomenon, which has the force of a moral truth, is confirmed in every aspect of the mid-Victorian scene. They were convinced of a steady improvement in the world. The complacent optimism of Macaulay, for instance, will allow of no possibility that everything in history is not

7

for the best. There was a universal belief that the parliamentary system would become the model of every other country in the world. More important still, the conversion of the heathen was to quicken and accelerate until all were saved. It was only in accordance with the same system of belief that they thought it wrong for the artist to pick and choose. His moral duty was to paint truthfully and exactly what lay before his eyes. This doctrine, as we shall see, was pushed to comical lengths by its extreme devotees. But their fanaticism, for it amounted almost to that, is the Victorian confession of faith. This time was the high tide of English prosperity and wealth. The world poured its riches into her lap; and both that world and those riches were acceptable in her eyes. This unashamed materialism, fortified by a religious belief that savours almost of hypocrisy, is behind the painting of realism as practised by the mid-Victorian artists. Ruskin, who taught these doctrines, was the phenomenon, we must remember, and not the creator of his age. Its philosophy would have developed independently of him. The Pre-Raphaelite painters owed nothing to him in the inception of their movement. *Modern Painters* is a mass of inchoate wonders which it is most difficult to read consecutively. It contains passages of writing which are unrivalled in English prose; but the whole book is a mountainous accumulation occasioned by something really inappropriate to its own purposes. The hero of *Modern Painters* was already an old man of seventy when the first volume was published. The other modern painters extolled, beside Turner, are men who are, by now, half forgotten. Prout and Clarkson Stanfield and Copley Fielding are, indeed, painters whom it is hardly worth while remembering. But the formation of the Pre-Raphaelite Brotherhood, done without knowledge or approval of Ruskin, might have been the exact creation of his ideals. If he, then, rallied to it with much enthusiasm, but without the energy which took him through seven volumes of *Modern Painters*, it is only because of the contradictions which were inseparable from Ruskin all through his confident but unhappy life. Like so much else in his career this is a pathetic instance of misguided faith.

It is difficult, now, not to see this same fault, only we use this word in its geological and not in its moral sense, in the ideals and the practice of everyone who subscribed to those tenets. But it was, at least, as we have said, a form of fanaticism and its fervencies were their support. The 'pictur'd morals' which had been invented by Hogarth, a hundred years and more ago, assume now a new importance. Every picture, more, even, than in the hands of Hogarth, has to tell a story; and, if the painting is nothing but a study of field flowers, a microscopic vision as if lying in the grass,

7. THE TOILET

H. Fuseli

Brinsley Ford, Esq.

8. THE RUNAWAY KNOCK

George Cruickshank

then, just as certainly, the message is one of confident faith and of the purpose and design that lie behind every manifestation of nature. Nothing but a fanatical belief could have produced such prodigies of labour as Holman Hunt's Hireling Shepherd (10), or Madox Brown's Work (11). Madox Brown, though, was steeped in the political creeds of his time, so that Work is his tribute to the manly dignity of labour. It does not count for nothing in this picture that Carlyle, whose *French Revolution* was as far-reaching in its effects as Ruskin's *Modern Painters*, is among the spectators who are watching the workmen. This painting, in fact, represents the moral revival, not in its aesthetic directions, but turned towards its humanitarian or social aspects. It is a propagandist picture, and its message is one of toil and its fatigues and rewards. The Blind Girl of Millais (1), which might be chosen as the other most important painting of the whole movement, has its moral message conveyed in sentimental form. All the beauties of nature surround the blind girl, but she is barred from them, since it is possible for the knowledge of a later generation to add to the point of the story, by an affliction which is inherited from sin. The fault of her parents has deprived her of sight. Millais, then, had created a dramatic or pathetic situation of which only half the meaning was apparent to him. But it was a discovery in dramatics, no less than a remarkable and beautiful picture. The unconscious touch of Ibsen in its theme gives it, indeed, a dramatic restraint which is the more telling.

These three paintings, The Hireling Shepherd, Work, and The Blind Girl have an importance which the prevailing taste for French paintings of that same time must not be allowed to obscure. If the rest of Millais and of Holman Hunt, and a good deal of Madox Brown, is absurd to us because of its empty sentiment and its inconsistencies in taste, these three pictures, at least, have a conscientious force of which only Courbet, perhaps, was capable. By no possible turn of taste could the three English painters in question be called great artists, but, just as surely, it cannot be denied that their three paintings are great pictures. They possess, within the limits of their decidedly pedestrian convention, an astonishing technical perfection. Their colours have lasted undimmed and undestroyed. Their elaboration of finish, if this be any criterion of judgement, is of a minuteness which it would be impossible to surpass. Truth and honesty could not be carried to a further point. They even possess a decided poetry, which is a thing quite apart from the crinolines or stove-pipe hats of their time. It is a poetry that is imbued in them owing to their close association to literature, and it is a literature which has become lyrical in those long moments. The Blind Girl has a Tennysonian association, but of that great poet in his

9

finer moods. The Hireling Shepherd, too, is a poetical conception; while we have already suggested that Carlyle has more connection with Work than his mere physical presence among the spectators painted in the background. Endless patience and tireless fidelity to fact have, on occasion, carried their practitioners to distances to which their inspiration could never have attained. Such is the case in another picture of that time, Brett's Vale of Aosta, a landscape which is, on every count, a most extraordinary performance. These exceptional occurrences have come to very ordinary men, when working with a force which is comparable to a religious belief, or a revelation. In the instances of Millais, Holman Hunt and Madox Brown, the explanation is more easy to understand. Millais was one of the most naturally gifted artists who have ever appeared in English art. His gift was comparable in scale and calibre to that of Gainsborough or Turner. There was nothing that Millais could not have accomplished, had his spirit been willing. He was a prodigy, possessing at twenty years of age, or less, more talent and its fulfilment than have been granted to almost any painter whom it is possible to remember. But Millais becomes, after this, one of the Fallen Angels of painting. His ignominious collapse, coming suddenly in the space of only a year or so, is unrelieved for nearly half a century more of life by a single spark, or by the merest glimmering of what he had once been, long before. There is hardly another parallel to this in the history of painting. This brilliant youth who had been the quintessence of all that poetical spirit implied in the Pre-Raphaelites, for Swinburne, be it remembered, was their great glory, this brilliant youth became the bad Academy painter personified. Strong drink or dissipation have never wrought havoc such as this. It might be described as a moral collapse taking the form of exaggerated moral observance. Millais must have considered himself as a faithful servant of the public, he was so determined never to offend them in either word or deed. He took the easy path of virtue and, having committed no aesthetic sins, hardly, in the end, comes up for judgement.

It is difficult, perhaps, to take recognition of the fact that the three paintings under discussion are, on the average, some eighty years old. Never again, during the remaining half-century of the Victorian period, were any pictures painted that could be said to belong to this monumental category. Whistler may occur to mind; but none of his paintings, as he would have been the first to admit, himself, are done in this spirit of patient seriousness. And it may be just because they are so lacking in sense of humour that they have achieved this solemn distinction. Perhaps the proper study of that whole age has yet to be written. It possessed, in such perfection,

9.　MAY MORNING ON MAGDALEN TOWER

W. Holman Hunt　　　　　　　　　　　*The Lady Lever Art Gallery, Port Sunlight*

10.　THE HIRELING SHEPHERD

W. Holman Hunt　　　　　　　　　　　*The Manchester City Art Gallery*

Ford Madox Brown   II. WORK   *The Manchester City Art Galler*

Ford Madox Brown   12. PRETTY BAA LAMBS   *The Ashmolean Museum, Oxford*

its own extremes of sublimity and bathos. Where else, and of what other period, could the following quotation be true?:

> ' I rode to see
> The church-restorings; lounged awhile,
> And met the Dean; was asked to tea,
> And found their cousin, Frederick Graham,
> At Honor's side.'

These few lines, from a poem by Coventry Patmore, give us the whole picture of mid-Victorian England in its refined and educated circles. Bathos could not be carried further, but a more complete picture is obtained than from most of the three-volume novels of that time. In fact, this quatrain —if it be a quatrain?—by Coventry Patmore is equivalent to all of Trollope reduced into an epigram. Neither can the present century afford to be too amused at it, for that period was the greatest epoch of English history and, now, it will never come again. Its conventions, since it has not long left us, are as strange and improbable to us as those of Louis XIV and his Court. So, perhaps, must every age appear in the eyes of its grandchildren. But its qualities, if they can be summed up in a phrase, would seem to have been a serious point of view and the taking of pains. It was conscientious effort, undertaken in the conviction that all things were for the best. Every enterprise to which the artist set his hand will serve to prove the truth of this generalization. It is only necessary to consider the extraordinary body of book illustrations for which the 'sixties are celebrated, and then ponder upon the pains and labour by which these complicated drawings were transferred to the wood. Frederick Sandys, or Pinwell, or Boyd Houghton, were certainly hard taskmasters to their engravers. But, also, the three-volume novel is symptomatic of the time; and, if we were to take the same theories further afield, we should find confirmation of a parallel existence, abroad, in the elaborate embroideries of notes, the tinsel and filigree and ornament of Liszt, and in the agonized searchings for the exact word by which Flaubert delayed, for so many years on end, the publication of his few masterpieces. These things are present, as well, in the coloratura of Verdi or Meyerbeer; in the exaggerated lengths of material necessary to make a crinoline; and in most of the useless and over-ornamented objects exhibited at the Crystal Palace in 1851. Returning to these shores again, it is apparent, then, that the realism of detail in The Blind Girl, or in Work, or in The Hireling Shepherd, is the direct and immediate symptom of its time in its most characteristic development, even though these three paintings were regarded derisively and with contempt at their first appearance. The Pre-Raphaelites had to suffer, in their early days, as much as Manet and the Impressionists were to endure a decade later, in the 'sixties. Unfortunately, the ludicrous lengths to which Holman Hunt carried his fidelity and the inexcusable failure of Millais make it hopeless to pursue the comparison any further. But within the first few years of their association the Pre-Raphaelites produced as many good paintings as could have been purchased at the *Salons des Refusées* of the Impressionists.

But if these three paintings that have been so long under discussion are the great works of the Victorian period, there are, as well, many lesser pictures that will leave, at the least, a pleasant impression upon our curiosity. The person, moreover, who compares them in all seriousness with those paintings that have been done in England during the twenty years that have elapsed since the War will have to admit to himself that the period from 1840 to 1860 was far from contemptible in the works of art that it produced. Rossetti, in spite of his technical shortcomings, had an influence second only to that of Ruskin. And since this impetus that was derived from him wrought its effects among less pedestrian minds than those to whom the moral teachings of Ruskin had appeal, it can be argued that Rossetti and not Ruskin was the genius of the hour. It was Rossetti who inspired Millais and Holman Hunt during their short terms of poetical afflatus. Ruskin only came to their defence when the paintings were on exhibition. He arrived late on the scene and signified his approval; but Rossetti had suggested the whole style and content of the movement. Pre-Raphaelitism must have been, in point of inspiration, the personal property and effects of Rossetti. Its doctrines happened to coincide with the multiple conclusions arrived at by Ruskin in his inchoate masterpiece. This was the spirit of the age working out its own ends and finding, in the course of that, parallel instances and more than one oracle to make its utterances.

It is to be expected, then, that this simultaneous expression should find its proof in the smaller accomplished facts. Such is the case on numerous occasions. There are, at least, three or four considerable painters in whom the movement came to full fruition of its teachings. John Brett, during the few years when he worked under the direct personal influence of Ruskin, produced The Stonebreaker (13) and The Vale of Aosta, two paintings to which the term a *tour de force* can really be applied. Arthur Hughes, another almost forgotten artist, painted some exquisite and touching pictures of sentiment. April Love (122) and Home from the Sea are singular and unique among a class of paintings that in every other case are too mawkish to be allowed serious mention. There is also an older painter, J. F. Lewis,

John Brett

13. THE STONEBREAKER

The Walker Art Gallery, Liverpool

works by whom can always impart something of a shock of discovery. He is a most interesting man, in minor ways, and a painter of scrupulous and unswerving fidelity. His best works, both in oil and in water-colour, remain in a category to themselves. And, finally, there is Richard Dadd, a painter about whom hardly a line has been written in any work of criticism. His tragic life, which is without precedent in the history of painting, where, at least, painters of his potential gift are concerned, puts Richard Dadd into a position of peculiar curiosity where the rare works by him, when they occur, are welcomed by his few admirers with a warmth of interest which is the criterion of his powers. It will be seen, in the course of this book, that this lost spirit, in the dimming of his faculties, arrived at a furious and despairing realism of imagination, since direct vision of life was denied to him by circumstances. He achieved, in a small way, some things that are astonishing and without parallel. There is hardly another instance in which fate has denied its fame to so cruel and undeserved an extent. Richard Dadd, as well, has an especial appeal to the most recent fashions in painting, so that it is perhaps a fortunate thing for his permanent reputation that he has been so little noticed. This *âme damnée*, so much more truly than Lautréamont, could be revived and allowed the light. But the seekers in the obscure and the sensational have, so far, neglected this treasure that is under their eyes.

This book will reach its end, most appropriately, with the mention of Tissot, who was forgotten for so long, and is now so popular. Tissot is last, but not least, of the painters of daily life. But, counting for less, it must be presumed, than the painters, there is the vast and unending treasure-house of the draughtsmen. In this, at any rate, the English school may bear comparison with the art of any other European nation. Our popular draughtsmen have no parallel in Holland or Spain, none in Italy, and only near rivals and not superiors in France. The great and ubiquitous Rowlandson is the first name that comes to mind, and since it is not possible to give him adequate space in our chapter that deals with the eighteenth century, this is perhaps the moment in which to enlarge upon his genius. There must be many who prefer him to Hogarth and are willing, because of their predilection, to condone the fact that no mere draughtsman can compete upon the same scale as the painter of large canvases. Rowlandson, however, has this prime merit that the tightness and constriction of Hogarth are altogether lacking in him. Hogarth is at his best when his canvases are most loaded with incident and detail, when the stillness of so many small objects in a crowded room, full of figures, makes us want a pin to drop, or some slight noise to break the silence. Rowlandson, by contrast, is flowing and alive with movement. Also, he has the physique, the robust liveliness, to altogether transcend the small limits of his convention. His drawings have a largeness of scale that is almost comparable to the canon of Rubens.

But, thinking of this, there are so many different Rowlandsons. He can be preferred in widely divergent moods. There are his parade pieces, of the type made familiar to us by the engraving of Vauxhall Gardens. This is the mood of Debucourt, and as good as that. The English and the French Review are two more drawings of that memorable sort. But there are, as well, in great number, his drawings of market-squares, and harbours and shipping wharves. These are crowded with hundreds of figures and have a boldness of design and a richness of imagination that become prodigious when we consider the quantity of them that he executed. There is a certain fundamental importance of architectural shapes, a sort of dramatic advantage taken by the artist over every opportunity, that put these large and crowded drawings into a category where Rowlandson has never been equalled. Drawings of this sort come and go in the memory. They are exhibited and sold; or they are in private possession and may often change hands. Thus, in twenty years' familiarity with his drawings, it is difficult to specify the best that have come under personal notice. A scene in the market-square at Antwerp stands out, though, in the memory; as do many astonishing drawings of this type collected at present in a gallery in Bond Street. There are, in general, military scenes, shipping scenes, landscapes with country houses, market-squares, courtyards of inns, interiors of dining-rooms, and a population of soldiers, pugilists, fishwives, and brawling sailors, large and blonde women, lawyers in bag-wigs, old schoolmasters, clergymen, university dons, etc., etc. His drawings of France or Flanders, belonging to this type, have generally a postchaise crowded with extravagantly dressed foreigners and a lumbering waggon full of friars. The perspective of the architecture, when this is the case, is certain to be of an excellence which demonstrates a lively interest on the part of the artist. Rowlandson, in fact, is never better than when there are fine and characteristic buildings for him to draw.

But there are, as well, the smaller drawings in which swifter effects are aimed at and achieved. Many of these are of surpassing beauty. It is difficult not to consider The Exhibition 'Starecase' at Burlington House (14) as his masterpiece. The headlong falling of those fat figures down the stairway, which, in itself, is a beautiful architectural conception, is given contrast by the leanness of some of the spectators who are looking on at and delighting in this descent into the abyss. And, indeed, as a design

14.   THE EXHIBITION "STARECASE"

Thomas Rowlandson   *University College, London*

15. THE UNLUCKY GAMBLER

Thomas Rowlandson

H. Reitlinger, Esq.

16. VISIT TO AN OLD ACQUAINTANCE

Thomas Rowlandson

H. Reitlinger, Esq.

17. THE RETURN

Thomas Rowlandson

J. L. Wright, Esq.

18. DRESSING FOR THE MASQUERADE

Thomas Rowlandson

Sir Edward Marsh

of tumbling and falling figures, controlled in their descent by principles of design and form, this drawing may be compared, without impiety, to the huge and gigantic Fall of the Rebel Angels, by Rubens, in the gallery at Munich. In addition, it is an inspired parody and among the wittiest drawings ever done. Another drawing of about this dimension is The Gardener's Offering (19), which is in the collection of Mr. Henry Harris. It shows a beautiful red-walled kitchen-garden and a range of glass-houses, in front of which the gardener gives a bouquet of flowers to a young woman. This drawing is in the atmosphere, if we can be understood, of the *Nozze di Figaro*. It is a wonderful and exquisite thing.

To many persons Rowlandson will be known chiefly for his plates to the *Three Tours of Doctor Syntax*. These were done late in his life, when nearly sixty years of age, and they represent, as does, indeed, *The Barber of Seville*, the pendant to that opera we have just mentioned, a sort of purposeful dwelling upon the century that had gone. The date, both of *Doctor Syntax* and of *The Barber of Seville*, is the same year, 1815. Both are clear products of the century before. They linger, with every symptom of delight, in the old conventions. They distil a kind of nostalgia of the past, not from the point of view of our own present, but by fixing the station of reminiscence just at the date of their own creation. It is the nostalgia of 1815 for the eighteenth century, and gives us, therefore, as through a transparency, the salient things connected in their minds with the dead century whose ends they all remembered. *Doctor Syntax* may be the most famous and popular of all the books that Rowlandson illustrated, but it is essential also to mention his *English Dance of Death*, two volumes which contain really magnificent drawings by his hand. The plates were done by Rowlandson as a series, and Thomas Combe, the author of *Doctor Syntax*, wrote his supremely uninteresting poem to accompany them. *The Dance of Life*, its sequel, is not so interesting. Neither is *The Adventures of Johnny Newcome in the Navy*, nor a most curious book, *The Adventures of Qui Hi*, a sort of East Indian Hudibrastic poem, with drawings in the Hindu style which are frankly very bad and only fit to adorn the labels of chutney bottles, to which, indeed, they bear a distinct affinity. On the other hand, Rowlandson drew illustrations to at least two more books of an excellence equal to anything that he accomplished in this branch of his art. These two books are *A Sentimental Tour in the Southern Provinces of France* and *Letters from Naples and the Campagna Felice*. The first contains some splendid street scenes at Avignon, swarming with fat Franciscan friars and a remarkable drawing of the arrival of a *diligence*, which as a composition has something of a quality of a Goya tapestry cartoon. The second of these two books, *Letters from the Campagna Felice*, is concerned with Naples. There are plates of popular Neapolitan life, a ball taking place in the gilded saloon of a palace, and a boat in the bay tossing under the stern of a splendid, carved vessel, while the cone of Vesuvius rises in the background. These drawings are taken from the sketches of someone else, for Rowlandson never went to Naples, but there is evidence in, for instance, the plate of the public letter-writer that he kept close to the original sketches, for this is a view of an existing scene not far from the San Carlo Opera House. It is curious, though, in this book devoted to Naples, to see that Rowlandson draws the same large, fair-haired women as in his scenes of England. Finally, it must not be forgotten in this mention of books illustrated by his drawings, that Rowlandson drew the plates, again from the sketches of an amateur, to *A Poetical Trip to Scarborough*; and, also, that he was responsible for the figures in *A Microcosm of London*, that immense Ackermann publication, for which the elder Pugin drew the architecture.

There remains the cheap and coarsely coloured Rowlandson, the Rowlandson of the popular print, issued chiefly by the firm of Thomas Tegg. These seem to have been drawn by Rowlandson late in his life, for most of them date from about 1808 to 1820. They must amount to several hundreds in number, and a complete collection, were that possible, would make an astonishing revelation of his powers. It is still possible, even now, to buy these prints for a sovereign apiece, or less; but apart from the large and rambling book by Joseph Grego, published nearly sixty years ago, there seems to be no authority upon them. There is no one to say which one of the prints is rare, or is easily met with; in fact, the information upon them is inaccurate and almost non-existent. Yet this, in many ways, is the essential Rowlandson. The scenes are never political caricatures. They are social satires of a ferocious character. The physiognomy is distorted, in goitrous, cretinous or drunken canon, and generally livid or purplish in hue. Hands and feet are monstrously distended. The scenes are old men lying on chairs with their bandaged legs propped up for gout; doctors examining appalling patients; an old father or uncle stumbling blindly along, while a young officer or a student kisses the daughter or niece and arranges their next meeting under the very nose of infirmity. Sometimes the scene is more ample; Wapping Stairs; Portsmouth Point and the crews of vessels celebrating; the French or English ordinary, two scenes, in contrast, in the dining-rooms of inns; old gentlemen looking through their glasses at the bathers; or some huge and swollen comedy of vulgarity, centred on a coarse play of words. These crudely coloured prints

Thomas Rowlandson

19.   THE GARDENER'S OFFERING

Henry Harris, Esq.

reach to a point of Japanese convention. They are as far-fetched, in fact, as any Sharaku or Utamaro. And, always, the accessories are sturdy and sensible in design. A great age of architecture and design still lives and is proved in their every detail. The whole body of these prints, as we have said, would be sensational and terrible in effect. Reality has seldom been seen by the artist through such a mirror of distortion.

If Rowlandson scarcely attempted political caricature it was because he left this to the hands of Gillray. This tremendous satirist was born in the same year, 1757, but he worked only and entirely for the printsellers. In the case of Gillray, again, the only authority is the eccentric Grego. The pursuit of Gillray through his caricatures becomes, then, a haphazard task made difficult by a lack of direction. It has, as well, all the obscurity of dead politics. His explosions of anger and contempt are so often impossible for us to follow. But Gillray, beyond any doubt, is the genius of caricature. A few of his masterpieces may be enumerated: A Connoisseur examining a Cooper is a cartoon of George III looking, by candle-light, at a miniature of Oliver Cromwell; Temperance enjoying a frugal Meal and A Voluptuary under the Horrors of Digestion are two contrasted studies of George III and the Prince Regent; The Middlesex Election speaks for itself; The King of Brobdingnag and Gulliver are studies of George III and Napoleon; L'Assemblée Nationale supposes the execution of the King and the proclamation of a Republic with Fox as First Consul, not without approval from the then Prince of Wales, part of whose figure appears in the corner; A Pic Nic Orchestra, Dilettanti Theatricals and Blowing up Pic Nics are three satires, in the last of which Sheridan appears as Harlequin. The above may be among the most famous of Gillray's caricatures, but indeed his more crowded plates reach to a degree of fantasy that has no equal among merely ephemeral productions. An extraordinary bite and invective is the special property of his line. This is in evidence when the caricatures are uncoloured; but the whirling phantasmagoria, when the plates are tinted, attains to the hugest scale. Distortion is used to its fullest extent, and every infamy and depravity attaches itself to the objects of his hate. Gillray is no sparer of women, and this trait, which a more lenient state has dismissed from under our eyes so that one-half of the world only is censured, doubles his potential venom and leaves him with no weapon of satire that he will not use. Nobody and nothing is forgiven by him. It would seem as though his imagination was spurred by his dreadful instruments into an insane excitement. The more elaborate of his caricatures transcend the ordinary human limits so that they exist only in the world of morbid fantasy. It is not surprising, in fact, that Gillray became deranged in his mind, helped in that by his extreme intemperance. The few last years of his life were passed, so we are told, in states of mingled imbecility and delirium. It is, naturally, his more extreme efforts in caricature that are the most interesting. His obsessions load and populate his stage, for they have the character, in fact, of nightmare pantomime. The unrealities become material and, for a moment, in defiance of every law of life, they play their incredible parts. It is upon these inspired occasions that we see this morbid fantasist in his true light as a genius of invention and elaboration. In these respects Gillray has no equal.

There is a tradition that the other genius of English caricature was called in by Mrs. Humphreys, the publisher and printseller of St. James's Street, in whose house Gillray had lived for so many years, in order that he should complete the plates upon which Gillray had been engaged until his illness made it hopeless for him to proceed any further. George Cruikshank, who was born in 1792, would have been at that time, in 1811 or 1812, some twenty years of age. It is certain, even, that he had seen and spoken to Gillray, and for these reasons the early work of Cruikshank is definitely in the idiom of Gillray. His caricatures of the Prince Regent, more especially the famous *Non mi Ricordo*, are in appendix, as it were, to Gillray. Perhaps the original Cruikshank appears for the first time in his travesties of the fashions, a series entitled Fashionable Monstrosities. These must be familiar to nearly everyone. The years from 1815 to 1825 were a time of mad fantasy in dress, fostered by the Prince Regent himself, in his character as the best-dressed man in Europe. The collection published under the name of Cruikshankiana, in 1830, contains a number of these; but the rest is Gillray, with so close a resemblance that the apprenticeship is most glaringly evident.

Just before this time Cruikshank had developed into more than one new direction. It is to be seen, first of all, in his etchings to *Peter Schlemihl*, from the German of La Motte Fouqué. These date from 1823, and they were followed immediately by his plates to *Grimm's Fairy Tales* and to *Grimm's Popular Stories*. These etchings, which were so much admired by Ruskin, are among the lesser masterpieces of the Romantic Movement. More especially, his drawings of the shadowless man, of the ghostly figure, for instance, who stoops down to fold and pick up his own shadow, in *Peter Schlemihl*, reveal the future Cruikshank of Fagin in the condemned cell. A year or two previously, *Life in Paris*, with its coloured plates and smaller woodcuts, had marked the culmination, as it were, of his early phase. These plates, it must be noted, like those drawn by Rowlandson to *Letters from the Campagna Felice*, were taken from sketches by an amateur.

Cruikshank had never been to Paris. In fact, like his predecessor Hogarth, he never went further abroad than a day trip to France, in this case to Boulogne. In 1826 the coloured aquatints to *Greenwich Hospital* were published. These show Cruikshank in another of his *fortes*, which consisted in his studies of sailors. The etchings to Dibdin's *Sea Songs* are more specimens of these. From this point it would be hopeless to attempt to keep pace with his tremendous output. Enough may be said, however, to establish the main lines of his development.

This proceeded into many directions at one and the same time. There are those, for instance, who would prefer the two series of *Mornings at Bow Street*, or *My Sketch Book*. On the other hand, the seventeen volumes of the Novelists' Library, consisting of his drawings to Smollett, Goldsmith, Fielding, Sterne, etc., etc., mark his first adventures into the historical style. For our own part, our predilection at this period is for *The Comic Almanack*, a most wonderful compilation of his wit and invention, which ran from 1835 until 1853. This contains an illustration for each of the months, as well as innumerable smaller drawings and decorations. London is to be seen in its true character in *The Comic Almanack*, for this is Cruikshank at his inimitable best. Any one volume seems to hold the present, as well as the dead past, of this smoky metropolis. We remember, particularly, August in London, with passers-by eating from the first oyster stall, a hoarding covered with posters, a London lamp-post—everything that is most characteristic of London. Then, again, there are the two series of *Sketches by Boz*, containing the immortal Early Morning in London. Equally, at this same time, Cruikshank's etchings to the *Life of Grimaldi* are our introduction to his admirable clowns and to his love of the Harlequinade. Cruikshank was a friend of Grimaldi and a member of The Crib, a club of clowns which used to meet at a room in a public-house at Sadler's Wells. And now, immediately, we arrive at the Cruikshank of Dickens. *Oliver Twist* is the memorial of this. In the meantime, his association with Harrison Ainsworth, brought the plates to *Windsor Castle*, *The Tower of London* and many other historical novels. Two more attempts in the manner of *The Comic Almanack* were *George Cruikshank's Omnibus* and the *Table Book*, both containing some of his best work, but doomed as failures. His final efforts, upon his old scale, were his etchings to *The Life of John Falstaff*, and the four volumes of his *Fairy Library*. This brings us to the year 1858, after which an alteration is to be noticed.

Cruikshank had become a confirmed teetotaller. This was to be the main interest of his life. He had already published, ten years before, *The Bottle* and *The Drunkard's Children*, two powerful and sinister series of propaganda for the cause. Now, at about the age of seventy, having taken lately to painting in oils, the smaller effects of which are to receive notice in the body of this book, he set to work upon *The Worship of Bacchus* (99), an immense composition containing hundreds of figures. It occupied two or three years of his life and, in spite of the attention that it attracted, was a failure from his point of view. It was to have been the culmination of his lifetime of work: instead, it was something of a fiasco. After this, Cruikshank did no more than supply an etched frontispiece, or an illustration or two, to various books of children's stories or fairy tales. These continued to appear over another ten or twelve years, until 1875, when he was eighty-three years of age. In 1878 he died and was buried in St. Paul's Cathedral, in that part of London which still contains the living embodiment of much that he drew. This, indeed, is the immortal London, which was old in his youth, more than a hundred years ago, and will never die.

This present book, which began with Hogarth, has had to continue with Rowlandson and could not end without a consideration of Cruikshank. There are some, indeed, to whom Cruikshank is the major English artist of the nineteenth century. The long span of his life covers the whole of the first three-quarters of that period. He remembered the eighteenth century and lived until just short of the eighteen-eighties. He even published a coloured print, attacking the Paris Commune of 1871 which might be in his Gillray manner of 1811, sixty years before. The drawings in illustration of his projected Autobiography, upon which he was engaged in the 'seventies, just before his death, are occupied entirely with the eighteenth-century scene of his childhood. In point of etching they amount to little more than casual, haphazard scratchings of his needle, but they are instinct with a childhood passed three generations before. Cruikshank has, it may be, a special appeal in this time when the essential London is being attacked and demolished on all sides. For his genius gives us, not only its appearance, but the entire population of its streets and houses. He is the delineator of London as surely as Canaletto or Guardi are the painters of Venice. But Cruikshank is many other things as well. He is among the first artists to attempt historical accuracy in their reconstruction of the past. The proofs of this are the seventeen volumes of the Novelists' Library, and his illustrations to Harrison Ainsworth. We must recapitulate, as well, his clowns, his sailors, the fantasies of his fairy stories, the whole corpus of his early Gillray manner, his *Life in Paris*, and some idea may be given of his protean activity. But there are, as well, all the sidelines of his talent, his drawings, for instance, for *Punch and Judy*, which are the last word upon that endless subject; or his terrible etchings to *A History of the Irish Rebellion*.

L. E. Lami

20.   SCENE IN BELGRAVE SQUARE

The Victoria and Albert Museum

L. E. Lami   21. SCENE AT LUDGATE CIRCUS   *The Victoria and Albert Museum*

These plates recapture the horrors of 1798, although it is certain Cruikshank never went as far as Ireland. It is said, in fact, that a trip to the chain pier at Margate was, for most of his life, the extreme limit of his travels from London. Everything that was necessary to his development as an artist was contained in London. It was enough for him to take his subjects, as did another great artist, Toulouse-Lautrec, in the narrowest possible radius and within a few minutes' walk of his home.

The personality of Cruikshank was, in its nature, the gift or talent of a prodigy. It found full expression within the space of a few square inches. He had a personal touch which, for the sake of this present book, we might compare, in degree, with that of Marcellus Laroon. It is unmistakable and not to be confused with that of any one of his contemporaries. He has a canon of proportion which is all his own and which we could term his convention. This corresponds, as a vehicle for his humour and observation, with the strange conventions of many popular comedians, with the immense shoes of Little Tich, or the bowler hat and black eyebrows of George Robey. It is only by thus establishing themselves out of the ordinary world that they can create their satires. Their segregation from the world puts them upon the plane of creation. In order to create character they have to be as disguised, and as extreme in that, as any priest or witch doctor. It is the same with the vehicle of the caricaturist. Only, in the case of Cruikshank, we are to assume that he was born with it, and that it was his natural channel of expression. Also, in the very nature of things, their touch, their identity must be at once known to the public. This is, in fact, another reason for the establishment of their peculiar convention. But his idiom was the natural speech of Cruikshank. Like a personal accent of the voice it was a thing which he could never part from. It informs each and every one of his undertakings. Fagin in the condemned cell is by the same hand, undisguised, that drew *Non mi Ricordo*, or the Monstrosities of the eighteen-twenties. His unchanged personality is his exceptional merit. It is Cruik-shank, in fact, who created his own peculiar world. That is his own personal property, and only by the labour of his hands could it come to life. It is, therefore, the true measure of his greatness.

This can be realized even more fully if we delay for a moment over his lesser contemporaries. A profitable instance is Hablot K. Browne, better known as 'Phiz.' It was 'Phiz' who drew most of the illustrations for *Pickwick*, and all the illustrations for *Nicholas Nickleby, Martin Chuzzlewit, Dombey and Son, David Copperfield, Bleak House, Little Dorrit, A Tale of Two Cities*; in fact, 'Phiz' was the illustrator of Dickens. These must be among the most widely circulated drawings in the world. They are known to everyone. The popular conception of the novels of Dickens has been much influenced by this visual interpretation of their characters, done with the approval, and often by the personal direction, of their author. But Hablot K. Browne, in spite of this, understates their message. He was an indifferent draughtsman gifted with a certain charm and a light and easy humour. He is never dramatic. If his engravings are compared with those by Cruikshank for *Oliver Twist* the inferiority of 'Phiz' is to be seen at the first glance. There were better artists than 'Phiz,' who, because they were not associated with a Dickens, never attained the fame that they deserved. Such was R. W. Buss, who drew the illustrations for the novels of Captain Marryat. Buss had a manner and a technique which become impressed upon the memory the moment one of his plates is seen. He had a particular bent for seafaring subjects, for adventures in distant parts. The illustrations of *Typee* and *Omoo*, those two tales of the South Seas by Herman Melville, should have been confided to R. W. Buss. He painted also some large subjects in oils, and it would be interesting, if almost certainly disappointing, to see these.

But, after Cruikshank, we come to one more personality who must remain something of an immortal where the life of England is concerned. This is John Leech. His dates—1817-1864—fit easily, and with more than enough to spare, within the life of Cruikshank, who was old enough to be his father. Leech is famous for his drawings for *Mr. Sponge's Sporting Tour*, *Handley Cross*, and the other sporting novels of R. S. Surtees. These are, though, in reality by far the weakest part of his output. It was for *Punch* that he did his best work. His three series of Life and Character reprinted from *Punch*, and his coloured etchings to *Punch's Pocket-Book*, an annual publication, are the masterpieces of Leech. In particular, his works in colour for the last-named volumes are entirely original things, forming the absolute mirror of their age. It is to John Leech that we must go if we want to know the exact look of the crinolined women at the seaside in the 'fifties. His drawings in black and white, for they are reproduced in woodcut, are no less true. But it is in colour that Leech surpasses himself, for this, it is evident, is the direction of his ambition, which was to be a painter. Had he lived there can be no doubt that he would have developed into a most remarkable artist. Of this culmination the first hesitant experiments are illustrated in an excellent specimen at a later page of this book.

After Leech comes Charles Keene. His work is of a later epoch, of the 'sixties and 'seventies. Keene was among the supreme draughtsmen of the English school, but his work, from its nature, is too ephemeral.

The illustration of a verbal joke requires too much rapidity, and an action which is too concise, to allow of detailed observation. His best drawings are miracles of grasp, they seize the passing situation and render it with a flashing rapidity which passes nearly out of drawing into calligraphy. His broad, hatching strokes of the pen convey the light and shadow upon the figures and are so satisfactory a pleasure in themselves that the point of the story is of no moment. These are living men and women, railway porters, cabdrivers, all and every character of the street. Any excuse for their existence is unnecessary. But Keene, also, for his own amusement, made most beautiful and delicate etchings. His work for *Punch* took up too much of his time. On occasion, when a coloured drawing by him was required for *Punch's Almanack*, or some similar publication, the latent possibilities in Keene become apparent. But, at the same time, Keene was too essentially a draughtsman in black and white. His accuracy in this, if not his charm, make him superior to Leech, but it may be doubted if he could ever have achieved in colour anything so wittily and triumphantly successful as Leech's Scarborough Sands (126), that painting of which an illustration has been promised in this book.

There still remains Phil May. He was the last of our great popular draughtsmen. His life, in its early and semi-starved days, had its sympathetic association with the stage. The young Phil May acted in pantomimes. It might be the life of Dan Leno, up to this point. But, before he was twenty years of age, Phil May was living by his pencil, making theatrical portraits, in fact. A spell of a few years spent in Australia, working for the *Sydney Bulletin*, developed his talent in its essential directions. There has seldom been such an economist in line. He removed everything superfluous and redundant until he could achieve wonderful effects of speed. Phil May was also so typical of his time that there are drawings by him which have affinities with Beardsley. His rendering of Cockney types is without a rival. The costermongers of Phil May are his speciality; but, as in the case of Leech and of Keene, if encouraged to work in colour, Phil May could excel himself and produce something so excellent that only a feeling of sadness is evoked at the thought of so much time spent at the drudgery of mere black and white. Phil May, in certain aspects of his economized drawing, as also in physical resemblance, has something in common with Picasso, the supreme artist of our own age. This may sound a far-fetched comparison but it is not untrue. Phil May, in mere calligraphy of drawing, has his supreme moments when he recalls a particular phase of Picasso; while any portrait of Phil May, putting aside the ravages of that malady or misfortune from which he suffered, must remind one, in physical type, of the great Spaniard. The *fin de siècle* is to be observed in strong degree in Phil May. His world of the saloon-bar was the same world, only insular and more robust, as that of his contemporary Toulouse-Lautrec. It is also to be recorded of Phil May that the vagaries of his temperament never obscured his character, which was that of the ideal painter, open, generous, and most affectionate to his friends. Aubrey Beardsley died of consumption, Toulouse-Lautrec of drink, Dan Leno of melancholia. What but a similar fate could be expected for their close and exact contemporary, Phil May? He died in 1904, belonging in entirety to the London between the Golden and the Diamond Jubilees.

It is the late 'eighties and all the 'nineties that we see before our eyes in Phil May. The old flower-sellers of the London streets are the living link between ourselves and that distant time. Their bonnets and shawls still speak to us of that. And, upon Sundays, in the fine summer weather of those far-off days, the costermongers in their yellow plush trousers sewn with buttons of mother-of-pearl danced with their wives and sweethearts in the feathered hats that we see in his drawings. Phil May, in fact, is the artist of Hampstead Heath, as he is of Petticoat Lane, or, equally, of the Strand. But, then, as well, we have the Phil May of Brighton or Scarborough and their odd characters, and the Phil May of the racecourse and the green-room. And Phil May, unlike nearly every other draughtsman whom we have mentioned, was as excellent when he worked abroad. His coloured drawings of Volendam, in Holland, are the only occasion upon which that most picturesque and much maligned fishing village has ever been rendered justice at the hands of an artist. With his death the long line of humorous draughtsmen was broken. That tradition which went back to Hogarth, and descended from him through Rowlandson and Gillray and Cruikshank, from Leech and Keene, was no more. It had lasted for the greater part of two hundred years.

This had been the popular or propaganda work of that movement which had for its chief ornaments the painters who are extolled in these pages. If pictured reality is to be our subject it would have been impossible to omit their names, for work such as theirs, which circulated into every direction, was the chief surety that principles of common sense guided the hands of our painters. And, long after we had ceased to have any artists worthy of the name, the tradition was carried on in the works of Leech and Keene and Phil May. Aubrey Beardsley was of this same race of artists, but in him the germs of disease brought a curious and exotic flavouring. Beardsley, and not Wilde, was the true genius of his period; but Beardsley, unfortunately, cannot enter within the scope of this book. His imagination

24

22.   THE INTERIOR OF A BUS

W. M. Egley   *Miss Blaker*

23. DIVIDEND DAY AT THE BANK OF ENGLAND

G. E. Hicks   *The Leicester Galleries*

24. THE LOWTHER ARCADE

Unknown Artist   *The Leicester Galleries*

bars him from this company. If, for that very reason, Beardsley is of the blood of Hogarth, the same course of thought will prove his disassociation from the other men who have been mentioned. It is to be remarked, though, in connection with the general trend of this book, how close to literature the genius of Beardsley approached. The exaggerated or transcendental form of his talent, grafted upon the ordinary stock which gave us Cruikshank, or Leech, or Rowlandson, comes back again into its true origin. Only a born writer could have attempted his *Venus and Tannhäuser*. Those few uncompleted pages, not intended in the least for the general public, are the only relics of a remarkable literary genius. This can be compared in its extraordinary elegance to *The Rape of the Lock*. It is, indeed, to Alexander Pope that this strange fragment has most resemblance, and it is a likeness of spirit, not a mere affected archaism. Both *Venus and Tannhäuser* and *The Rape of the Lock* are the work of young men. They were twenty-four years of age when their respective masterpieces were achieved. Both of them, also, were of precarious health. A sort of Chopinesque delicacy is, therefore, to be expected of them, but the exquisite refinements of their diction transcend most other things in our language. *Venus and Tannhäuser* is incomparable and, as yet, unrecognized for the work of art that it is. This recognition it may never receive, for the reasons which have made it impossible for the book to be openly published. But this conclusion to our subject has its peculiar and absorbing interest. Our thesis began and ends in literature. The 'pictur'd morals' which were the invention of Hogarth come back into literature in this decadent work of a Flavian or Silver Age. It is the proving of this long race of artists, having been born in the acted drama, that they should come to their end in this way. We will repeat the words of Hogarth: 'I wished to compose pictures on canvas similar to representatives on the stage; and further hope that they will be tried by the same taste, and criticized by the same criterion. . . . I have endeavoured to treat my subject as a dramatic writer; my picture is my stage, and men and women my players, who by means of certain actions and gestures, are to exhibit a dumb show.'

This intention was carried out in complete success by its originator and inventor. There is nothing in the whole range of our subject that can compare with the series of 'pictur'd morals' by Hogarth. So many discoveries reach to their highest pitch of development in the hands of the first pioneer. The art of printing was never so beautiful as within a few years of its invention; no subsequent virtuoso, we may feel certain, has played the violin as did Paganini, or the pianoforte as did Liszt. Hogarth, in fact, who invented and excelled in the Conversation Piece, was not less eminent in the painting of genre, in the rendering of incident or anecdote. He painted, in this, to a great audience; the private patronage of rich families was a small thing compared to this, and, as well, there was the revenue to be derived from the sale of his engravings. Through this double appeal his fame was universally disseminated. But no one who came after him had quite the ability or the energy so completely to capitalize his talent. This, certainly, would have been the last thing to expect of George Morland. The opportunity could only have come again with the Pre-Raphaelites; but so daring in their days were the innovations that they practised that no engravings of their pictures were called for. Holman Hunt, or Millais, possessed all the necessary industry and patience. What they lacked was the immediate popularity of Hogarth. For, owing to some reason which it is not easy to determine, Hogarth seems never to have met with opposition in his early career.

CHAPTER II

WILLIAM HOGARTH

It is no mere accident, perhaps, that made the Conversation Piece into one of the prides or specialities of English painting. Some excuse or convention was necessary, and, once this was established, our native-born painter could enter without more ado into a domain which tradition had reserved for the foreigner, for the Italian, the Fleming, or the Dutchman. But such is only the superficial aspect; the real reason is our great literary tradition. That descends, need it be said, from the universal genius of Shakespeare; and, in a truth and proportion which are only diminished by the difference in their stature, all our painting goes back to and depends from Hogarth. His 'pictur'd morals' form an enormous body of work, in comparison with which his few, but excellent, Conversation Pieces are but the efforts of his leisure moments, contrived and designed to please. His moral pieces were his serious purpose. They were the means by which his fame was spread, in engravings, into every country of Europe.

Everyone, at the mention of Hogarth, will think of his Rake's Progress or his Marriage à la Mode. They are the popular measure of his achievement. These were, in every sense, his original inventions. Hogarth was the earliest person in English painting to compose upon this elaborate scale. But his own words, written in a preface to which he set his hand, will explain his motives with a directness which cannot be misunderstood. 'Portrait painting was not sufficiently profitable to pay the expenses my family required. I therefore turned my thoughts to a still more novel mode, viz., painting and engraving modern moral subjects, a field not broken up in any country or any age. . . . I wished to compose pictures on canvas similar to representations on the stage; and further hope that they will be tried by the same test, and criticized by the same criterion. Let it be observed, that I mean to speak only of those scenes where the human species are actors, and these I think have not often been delineated in a way of which they are worthy and capable. . . . I have endeavoured to treat my subject as a dramatic writer; my picture is my stage, and men and women my players, who by means of certain actions and gestures, are to exhibit a dumb show. . . . This I found was most likely to answer my

27

purpose, provided I could strike the passions, and by small sums from many, by the sale of prints which I could engrave from my own pictures, thus secure my property to myself.' In the advertisement of A Harlot's Progress, and in more than one of his other plates, Hogarth speaks of himself as the 'author,' not the 'artist.' He seems to have conceived of himself as a 'comic writer,' in that superlative sense in which that phrase could be applied to Shakespeare, to Dryden, or later, and altered considerably in its conditions, to Dickens. It is in this company, we may say without presumption, and not in the society of Gainsborough, of Turner, or of Constable, that Hogarth would have himself remembered. He thus conforms most strictly to our native genius, without the extraneous influences of foreign fashion, or those half-successes which are the reward of tireless experiment. Hogarth was content with the utmost exploitation of those principles which he had formulated for himself early in his life. He worked in this quarry until its last veins were exhausted. Truth to life, which was his desired aim, he achieved not so much by the fidelity of his representation as by every detail in his anecdote, by the aptness of every small incident that he depicted. Hogarth, in the course of these pages, will yield us a hundred opportunities of pointing to these minutiæ of his imagination. He was as fertile in these corroborating inventions as Brueghel, a painter who from not dissimilar beginnings became in middle age, and not long before he died, one of the greatest of European painters. Hogarth, it is manifest, could never rise to those heights, but the full achievement of Hogarth is equal, at least, to the early Brueghel, and this comparison is no inconsiderable compliment, as the genius of Brueghel climbs slowly into its prominence among the great painters of the world.

But the mention of his characters as playing their parts in a 'dumb show' makes it necessary, in warning, to place apart and out of our context the actual theatrical subjects that Hogarth was to paint. Such, for instance, is that admirable scene from *The Beggar's Opera*, now in the Tate Gallery. This is one of the finest of Hogarth's early paintings, but it falls into a category of pictures that should form, one day, a separate study to itself, along with the admirable theatrical scenes of Zoffany and de Wilde. They can have no place here, among these 'pictur'd morals,' even if that term is given its widest application in order to include genre paintings of every scope and variety. Theatrical paintings belong to a world to themselves into which it is a pity to enter, unless it be to conduct a separate enquiry into their merit. Our field is already, therefore, restricted by their absence. For this is to be the fundamental Hogarth, the Rake's Progress, the Marriage à la Mode, in fact his moralities generally.

William Hogarth

26. MARRIAGE À LA MODE: THE BREAKFAST SCENE

The Tate Gallery

27. MARRIAGE *À LA MODE*: THE DEATH OF THE COUNTESS

William Hogarth   *The Tate Gallery*

28. THE RAKE'S PROGRESS: IN BEDLAM

William Hogarth   *The Soane Museum*

Of these the quantity is prodigious. The Harlot's Progress, the Rake's Progress, and Marriage à la Mode, alone make a total of twenty paintings. To follow these series through their different stories, item by item, would take up a fair-sized volume to itself. For the utmost detail of anecdote has been lavished upon every incident depicted. If there is a picture hanging upon the wall its subject points the moral, or is a satire upon the play of the figures. No detail is accidental or allowed its entrance without the weight of some meaning upon it. But the robust strength of Hogarth's personality survives this laborious stressing of the legend. It is only occasionally, or when the series becomes extended into too many pictures, that this accumulation of incident becomes wearying. The effort of looking back through the four or five pictures of a series in order to hunt down some piquancy of narration may end in a quandary as to whether this necessity can find inclusion in the art of painting. Each picture, in fact, of the Marriage à la Mode is better examined in isolation by itself and without consideration of what may come before or after it in the series. Otherwise, the subjects are more easy to understand and appreciate in engraving. They are crowded illustrations; and, if we did not know the contrary to be the fact, it would be no surprise to hear that Hogarth had first invented them as engravings or illustrations and afterwards made the oil paintings.

A Harlot's Progress, in six pictures, is the earliest attempt of Hogarth into this direction where he was to find his fame. It dates from 1731, when Hogarth was thirty-four years of age. Up till this time, having finished his apprenticeship as an engraver upon silver, and made many engravings for books—the best of them a set of twelve plates for *Hudibras*—his energies had been devoted mainly to small portraits and portrait groups, or Conversation Pieces. But, also, he had already painted his spirited picture of the Wanstead Assembly, as well as the aforementioned group from *The Beggar's Opera*. It is, in fact, his maturity. The scene from *The Indian Emperor*, the finest and most successful of his Conversation Pieces, dates from exactly this time. It is contemporary with A Harlot's Progress. The heroine, named appropriately Mary Hackabout, is the centre of the following scenes: I. Her arrival in London; II. She quarrels with her protector; III. She is apprehended by a magistrate; IV. Beating hemp in Bridewell; V. Her death; VI. Her funeral. These titles are sufficient indication of the unfolding of the plot. Not a few characters of the time are said to be represented in this rogue's gallery of the reign of George II. The notorious Colonel Charteris and his crony or familiar, Mother Needham, appear, or so it is said, in I.; two famous quack doctors of the day in V., and a clergyman of evil repute with another well-known procuress in the last picture of the series. Characteristic of Hogarth's minutiæ of detail are the Jew's bread used as a fly-trap in V., and, hardly less nauseating, the sprigs of yew hung up in the room to prevent infection in the last plate of all. A Harlot's Progress is, as we have said, the earliest of Hogarth's 'pictur'd morals,' and it lives in the memory, we must confess, more as a set of engravings than in terms of oil painting.

There is decided improvement in this respect with A Rake's Progress, painted and engraved in 1733-35. This consists of no fewer than eight scenes; but two of them at least are paintings of a high order. The whole series proceeds as follows: I. He takes possession; II. His Levée; III. He revels; IV. Goes to Court; V. He marries; VI. He gambles; VII. In the Fleet Prison; VIII. In Bedlam. The painting of the Levée (29) and the scene in Bedlam (28) are two of Hogarth's masterpieces. Scarcely inferior is the scene of revelry (30). In the Levée, the Rake has found his place in the fashionable world of Italian musicians and opera singers. A French dancing master, who is also a violinist, struts and capers before him; an older man in a full-bottomed wig sits, with his back to us, at the harpsi-chord trying over an opera which is entitled *The Rape of the Sabines*, while the rest of the room is filled to overcrowding with a French horn-player, a boy who holds a punch-bowl and a riding-whip, and a mass of busybodies all intent on making money out of this rich, young dude. The rake himself, very overdressed, seems almost lost in midst of them; that is to say, his scatter-brained features are rendered to perfection and in a prominence which is the more noticeable because he is the chief person in the painting and it is to him that all these varied characters are paying their court.

The scene of drunken revelry, III., is a splendid dramatic composition full of life and animation. It is to be noticed here, as other writers upon Hogarth have pointed out, that even in painting the most dissolute persons the ugliness of the attendant or minor actors is always counterbalanced by the beauty of some of the chief performers. In this instance, two, at least, of the denizens of this low tavern are remarkable for their good looks. And, as we look at this painting, we find ourselves preferring it even to the scene just described. For this is most definitely a picture. It is a work of art and no longer a mere illustration.

The eighth, and last, of the series shows us the Rake in Bedlam. This is a truly terrifying conception. He lies, nearly naked, and obviously stupefied at his surroundings, in a large room or hall in which the inmates of this terrible place play their delusions before our eyes. The very sound of the word Bedlam is a thing of horror: it is horrible in its mere sound, that is to say, as well as in its associations. This could find no more wonderful interpretation than in this, the painting that we are discussing. And, as a relief to the ugliness and squalor all around, partly, also, to point a moral by their indifference, or even gentle amusement at what they see, two beautiful young women, the one whispering into the other's ear, pass through the scene.

Such is the Rake's Progress. It must be familiar in its essentials to everyone who has had the curiosity to follow Hogarth from the mere fact of his name into the performances of his hand. This will be more true still of Marriage à la Mode, with which we will deal straightaway, so that the less familiar paintings of Hogarth can then receive our undivided attention. Marriage à la Mode, then, as to his engravings as well as to the pictures from which they were taken, was completed by 1745. It consists of six paintings: I. The Contract (25); II. The Breakfast Scene (26); III. The Scene with the Quack Doctor; IV. The Toilet Scene; V. The Death of the Earl; VI. The Death of the Countess (27). Of these the best, there is little question, are the second and the last. The opening picture of the series shows us the old peer, 'Lord Squanderfield,' sitting, stricken with gout, his crutches by his side, pointing proudly to his family tree upon the floor by his feet. His architects and builders are grouped round him and the new Palladian house that he is building appears in a view out of the window. The marriage between his son and the daughter of a rich, plebeian city merchant has just taken place, and the young pair, in an agonized indifference, are shown in the corner of the room. A couple of dogs, below them, are in cruel parody upon their lack of animal spirits. This careful symbolism in even the smallest detail is carried down to the lighted candle, with a 'thief' showing clearly in its flame, which waits for Lord Squanderfield's seal upon the marriage papers until he has done with his architects and builders.

The Breakfast Scene follows upon this. Here, in the careful words of Sir William Armstrong, the husband has 'returned from some independent nocturnal expedition.' He is a picture of dissipation, and his wife of lassitude. The room, which may have been meant for a satire upon the style of William Kent, impresses us with its fine proportions and air of culture and civilization. A delightful invention over which Hogarth must have laughed a lot is the combined clock and candle sconce upon the wall. This is the best instance imaginable of mixed metaphors. The ormolu clock has a china cat sitting upon it, while the brass twigs and leaves with which it is surrounded have great fishes swimming among them. But perhaps this painting takes its high place among Hogarth's works by reason of its comparative emptiness. In all this large room there are only four persons to be seen. The fourth of these pictures, the Toilet Scene, is much overdone in this respect. We like better the Scene with the Quack Doctor, with its curious retorts, its levers and its cog-wheels, though the actual significance of this painting is difficult to follow and has baffled most of its interpreters. But the Death of the Countess, which is the end of the Marriage à la Mode, is, once again, Hogarth in the height of his inspiration. It must be remarked that this picture does exactly resemble a scene upon the stage. The figures are all in arrested attitudes, as for the fall of the curtain. This image is corrected, so to speak, and brought back into actuality by the view of Old London Bridge out of the window with its leaning, toppling houses. The Countess, who has poisoned herself with laudanum, has her infant daughter held up to kiss her. A slatternly nurse is slobbering or crying. The doctor and servants are indifferent, but the Countess' father, the City merchant with an expressionless face, holds her hand and looks at her wedding-ring. In the corner, by the open window, a dog that is little better than a living skeleton has climbed up to the table and licks in ghastly fashion the half-eaten calf's head which is left over from the meal. Such, in brief, is the Marriage à la Mode. Its details could be enlarged upon; but it may be said of the Marriage à la Mode that either it is known, in which case too close an examination would be wearying, or else the complete explanation and unfolding of the plot would leave, in the end, an impression that these are anything but paintings. This, it has perhaps been sufficiently stressed, is not at all the truth.

By the date at which these canvases were completed Hogarth was nearly fifty years of age. There will be, in fact, many more of his pictures of which mention is overdue, if they are to be taken in chronological order. One of the most important of these is the Southwark Fair of 1733 which, as these lines are written, has come up for auction by order of the Duke of Newcastle. This is a full-sized canvas crowded with figures and possessed of all the bustle and animation of a Bank Holiday on Hampstead Heath. It is a typically Cockney gathering: the times have altered, but not the spirits of the fair. But, unlike a modern holiday, Southwark Fair continued for a fortnight, and this gave Hogarth enough time to crowd and overload his composition with many dozens of figures and as much relevant detail as can be seen in an early Brueghel. At the same time, it is not of Brueghel that we are reminded in Southwark Fair; there is nearer contact to Jan Steen. It is between Jan Steen and one of the winter *Kermesses* of Avercamp, though this is a resemblance only of spirit and not of fact, for Southwark

29. THE RAKE'S PROGRESS: HIS LEVÉE

William Hogarth

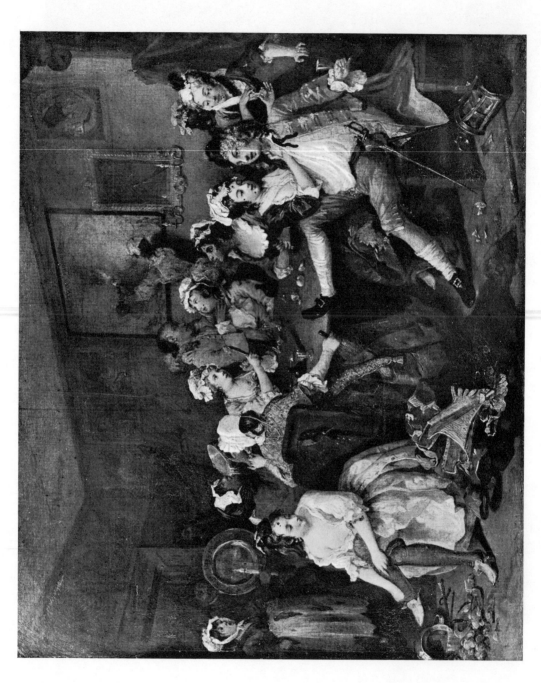

30. THE RAKE'S PROGRESS: HE REVELS

William Hogarth

Fair was a fine-weather carnival; the trees are in full leaf. Every kind of entertainment is in progress. Two theatrical companies in *The Siege of Troy* and *The Fall of Bajazet*, as well as a harlequinade, are playing; there are giants, conjurers, rope-walkers, prize-fighters, the 'curious Indian birds' of Mr. Fawkes, a waxwork of the whole Court of France, and, in the foreground, in midst of the crowd, a beautiful drummer girl beating a tattoo, as in *Petrouchka*, while her companion, in buskins and plumed helmet, is taken away by a pair of bailiffs. Near by, a black boy blows a trombone, and a terrible little Savoyard, with a performing monkey and some dancing dolls, plays a bagpipe. The spectators look idly on, stupefied by the general din, while the *Fall of Bajazet* is literally interpreted by the collapse of the hustings and the ignominious tumbling of the actors into the crowd. This touch, which compares with the 'drolleries' of Brueghel, perhaps rather mars the serious intention of the painting. It is a rich mine of detail and of character but not a great work of art.

A comparison, which is inevitable, must be drawn between this picture and the much later March to Finchley. The subject is the march of the Guards towards Scotland during the 1745 Rebellion. This is full of little items of observation; the pair of pipe-sucking crones in their cart, the faces at every window in the public-house, the universal pilfering and stealing under cover of patriotic feeling. Innumerable little jokes and tricks are playing through the crowd, the detection of which in the painting may have made the proof to its admirers that this was one of the greatest pictures ever done. On the other hand, its faithfulness to the Cockney crowd of that time apart, this canvas has not the importance of design which cannot be denied to Southwark Fair. And, indeed, for his portrayal of life in London there are designs by Hogarth that are more satisfactory than the March to Finchley; from the series of Industry and Idleness there is the splendid Lord Mayor's Procession, engraved but never painted, and in his early plates in *Hudibras*, the Burning of Rumps at Temple Bar is a terrifying and sinister conception with a quality as work of art that the March to Finchley does not possess.

We come now, however, to many paintings in which the great and true Hogarth is revealed as distinct from Hogarth the purveyor to the public; Southwark Fair and the March to Finchley were so many diploma pieces meant to attract attention because of their hundred relevancies and little tricks. They are crowd scenes, and it is not often that a crowd makes a composition as a work of art. The Strolling Actresses and the Four Times of the Day all date from 1738. The engravings of these five pictures were issued together and at the same time, so that the actual paintings will have been the work of the previous months. The first of these subjects represents a company of strolling actresses dressing in a barn. It is a conception of astounding force and vigour. Walpole says of it that 'for wit and imagination without any other end it is the best of all his works.' In fact, the Strolling Actresses is a work of art without too many minor relevancies and allusions. The Strolling Actresses may remind one, in some distant way, of the frescoes of Giulio Romano at Mantua. This is not a banquet of the Gods; but, at least, the Strolling Actresses are dressing for heroic roles. The company of 'barnstormers' have every classical myth in their repertory. Flora, Diana, Jupiter, Ganymede, Aurora, are all dressing under the wooden rafters. It is a satire upon the pretensions and poverty of the players; while, at the same time, there may be more talent here than among the fashionable Italians whom Hogarth so despised in the London opera. As ever, even in the most ferocious of his inventions, there are some women remarkable for their beauty. More than one writer has commented upon the exquisite prettiness of the leading lady of the troupe. It is probable that, as Walpole said, this was the masterpiece of Hogarth; but, most unfortunately, the picture was destroyed by a fire at Littleton, in Middlesex, in 1874, so that only the engraving is left by which to judge of its merits.

The Four Times of the Day are a set of four small paintings, all of which represent scenes in London. The first is an early winter morning at Covent Garden. This is probably the best of the series. It bears, even now, an astonishing resemblance to this part of London. The market has begun. A clock over the portico of St. George's gives the hour as just on eight o'clock. Some market-women have lit a fire of sticks; but the rest of the people astir in the cold are all revellers from Tom King's coffee-house, a low shed with its roof fringed with icicles, built below the church; except for a thin, unpleasant-looking old maid with her foot-boy shivering behind her, pinched with the cold, one hand in his pocket and the other thrust hopelessly into the lapels of his coat. This old maid, who taps her mouth with her fan and dangles keys and scissors from her waist, is said by tradition to have been an aunt of the painter. She is certainly one of the most ill-favoured of all his gallery of characters. But it is not so much the personalities of this picture as its portraiture of London that is important. There are, even in King Street, Covent Garden, two or three of the houses still standing, and there is even the Hawksmoor portico of St. George's, burnt down more than once but rebuilt in the same pattern. If this tangible evidence were removed, as it soon may be, this picture would still be Covent Garden, a part of London that has a character as strong and decided as the Piazza of St. Mark's or the Roman Forum.

William Hogarth   31.   AN ELECTION ENTERTAINMENT   *The Soane Museum*

32. CANVASSING FOR VOTES

William Hogarth

Morning is an especial favourite, but its three companion pictures are scarcely inferior. They represent a congregation coming out at noon from the French Chapel in Hog Lane, St. Giles' (2); a citizen and his wife walking back from Sadler's Wells on a warm summer evening; and a Restoration Day bonfire, at night, near Charing Cross. Noon has delightful and characteristic touches. A kite has been caught by its tail and dangles down upon the red bricks of the chapel; a black man is embracing a milkmaid; a little boy who has rested his pie-dish too clumsily upon a wooden post bursts into a paroxysm of tears, while a beggar-girl takes profit from the opportunity to pick up and eat the fragments out of the gutter; but the real delight of this picture is in the young Frenchman in all the coxcombry of fashion, in the overdressed fat boy with bag-wig, court suit, and sword at his side, and in the back view, beyond, of an extraordinary child waddling away, dressed in the height of fashion, his wig crowned with a hat of unbelievable shape. These figures are worthy of his inimitable Taste in High Life. This is the eternal Hogarth, who is immortal because he gave such life to one particular moment. His pictures of his own times are, on such occasions as this, the heightened truth, they are truth transcendentalized, and this is immortal and is the truth of all occasions.

The Gate of Calais (4), one of the best known of Hogarth's engravings, has its origin in the large oil painting of 1748, now in the National Gallery. It is also known as the Roast Beef of Old England. This, in fact, with Southwark Fair and the March to Finchley, is one of the most important of his isolated paintings. It is not related to any series, and has neither forerunner nor sequel. The subject is something so typical of the painter's personal character that it would be easy to think the incident apocryphal and only invented in order to suit him with the anecdote. It is best described in the words of Walpole, written in a letter to Sir Horace Mann, under date of 15th December 1748: 'Hogarth has run a great risk since the peace (of Aix la Chapelle); he went to France and was so imprudent as to be taking a sketch of the drawbridge at Calais. He was seized and carried to the Governor, where he was forced to prove his vocation by producing several *caricaturas* of the French; particularly a scene of the shore, with an immense piece of beef landing for the Lion-d'argent, the English inn at Calais, and several hungry friars following it. They were much diverted with his drawings, and dismissed him.' This was, in fact, the only occasion upon which Hogarth ever ventured abroad. So typical an instance of insularity as Dr. Johnson got at least as far afield as Paris and Versailles; but Hogarth set the limit to himself at Calais. It is easy

35

to imagine, without the necessity of being told, how scornful was his attitude toward anything and everything foreign. 'He pooh-poohed the houses, the furniture, the ornaments, or spoke of them openly with scornful opprobrium. In the streets he was often clamorously rude. A tattered boy, or a pair of silk stockings with holes in them, drew a torrent of imprudent language from him.' But this account of the incident by a malicious biographer finds corroboration in Hogarth's own words, or some approximation to them, as related in the Ireland MSS. 'The next print I engraved was the Roast Beef of Old England, which took rise from a visit I paid to France. The first time an Englishman goes from Dover to Calais he must be struck with the different face of things at so little a distance. A farcical pomp of war, pompous parade of religion, and much bustle with very little business. To sum up all, poverty, slavery, and innate insolence, covered with an affectation of politeness, give you even here a true picture of the manners of the whole nation.' After his arrest, while making the sketch of the Calais Gate, Hogarth was confined to his lodgings till the wind changed for England and a couple of guards were then provided to convey him on shipboard; nor did they quit him till he was three miles from shore. 'They then spun him round like a top, on the deck; and told him he was at liberty to proceed on his voyage without further attendance or molestation. With the slightest allusion to the ludicrous particulars of this affair, Hogarth was by no means pleased.' It is evident from this that the humour of the episode was of mutual operation, and that as to the one aspect of it Hogarth was as blind as he was alive to the other.

The Gate of Calais is a picture that is instinct with the personality of Hogarth, both in its strength and in its numerous weaknesses. Its humours are obvious and by no means over-refined. It is a big, burly composition, like the short, comic interlude from one of Shakespeare's plays. Only there is none of that divine impartiality where Hogarth is concerned. He is entirely absorbed and involved in his temporary characters. It is even irresistible for him to drag in a tattered Highlander and a squinting Irishman, two starving remnants of the Jacobite Rebellion of the '45. In the invention of Hogarth there is no such thing as a figure put in to close a composition. All of the actors have some purpose to fulfil. He is at the opposite pole of difference from Verrio or Laguerre, from the painters of sprawling figures for a ceiling.

We have arrived now at the maturity of Hogarth. It is, therefore, unfortunate for our purposes that Beer Street and Gin Lane should have been created only as engravings and not in the form of oil paintings, for they are the greatest and most effective creations of his hand. They are

William Hogarth

Sir Edmund Davis

33.   THE STAYMAKER

William Hogarth

35. AFTER

Thorsten Laurin, Esq.

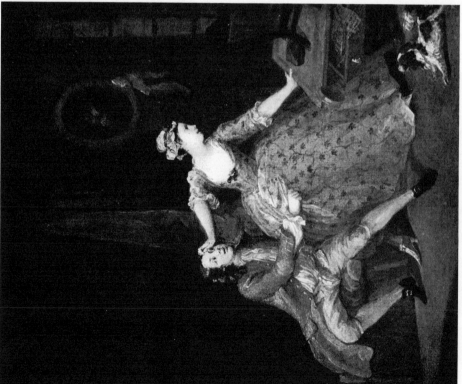

34. BEFORE

William Hogarth

Thorsten Laurin, Esq.

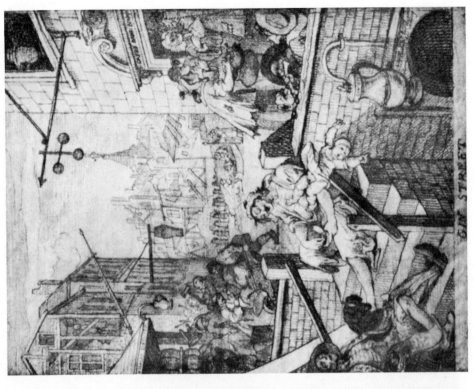

37. GIN STREET

William Hogarth

36. BEER STREET

William Hogarth

William Hogarth

38.   A DANCE AT THE WANSTEAD ASSEMBLY

The Borough of Camberwell, South London Art Gallery

dated 1751; and the Four Stages of Cruelty are works of the same year. Red-chalk drawings for all six of these engravings are still in existence (36, 37). This is the Cockney Hogarth in a mood which relates him very closely to George Cruikshank, the other great delineator of London. All six of these subjects, which have human cruelty and folly as their theme, are a revelation of the sordid and horrible. The human beings depicted in them are of a race which, in France, was to gather, at the end of the century, round the tumbrils. They are the mob of the Revolution; and why nothing of that kind was to happen in London must puzzle the mind of anyone who looks, shuddering, at their fearful physiognomy. Yet this is London completely personified, as we are reminded, even in the scene of the gin-sodden mother, and the beggars gnawing at a meat bone, by the white spire of St. George's, Bloomsbury, with its statue of George II, sceptre in hand, on Hawksmoor's version of the Mausoleum at Halicarnassus, rising into the air above the pawnbroker's sign and the tottering houses. Beer Street, too, has for background what would appear to be the white spire of St. Giles-in-the-Fields. Perhaps Gin Lane and Cruikshank's early morning scene in *Sketches by Boz* have more of the essential character of London than any other works that we can discover. This is London— London, the capital city of England, with its slums, its spires of white Portland stone, and the Lord Mayor and his gilded coach not far away, coming from the banks and the merchant houses.

Another print by Hogarth dating from the same time is the Cockpit. This is a thing of utmost verve and spirit. The audience are wonderfully contrasted in their types. Sordid excitement has never been better depicted, while the design of the composition itself is a superb oval following the shape of the arena. The line of spectators seen from their backs, in the foreground, is lifelike and masterly. As for the arena itself, its emptiness, compared with the small shapes of the two fighting cocks, is filled with an invention that is characteristic of Hogarth. This is the shadow of a defaulter, for his shadow only is seen, who, according to the usage of this violent place, has been drawn up to the ceiling in a basket. He is dangling his watch in his hand as a bait to satisfy his creditors. His ghost looms in its importance upon the white light of the arena and almost over-shadows the excitement of the fight. It is also, where the shadow of the actual watch is concerned, a sort of suggestion of the gallows with a figure dangling from it, in parable of the criminals who were certainly among the crowd. We shall see that this device of a shadow was used again by Hogarth.

It comes, indeed, into the culminating picture of the last great series that he undertook. These are the Four Pictures of an Election. They were completed by 1755 and the prints of them published during the four ensuing years. It so happens that these paintings, which were once the property of Garrick, have found for more than a century past a congenial resting-place in the Soane Museum in Lincoln's Inn Fields. There they may be seen, ingeniously arranged, on a series of sliding panels or compartments. The house of Sir John Soane, the last of our great line of architects, is a curious oasis in the noisy desert of neo-Georgian London, and certainly these four paintings by Hogarth are to be appreciated here as they would be in no other museum or picture gallery of the Metropolis. The four subjects are An Election Entertainment (31), Canvassing for Votes (32), Polling at the Hustings, and Chairing the Members. The first of these pictures is much more elaborate in composition than was usual with Hogarth. At first sight, it impresses not so much by accumulation of detail as by this surcharged and reinforced pattern of figures. This is not often the case in Hogarth. It occurs in the Scene from *The Indian Emperor*, the best of his Conversation Pieces, which is a better picture than this, but there is no painting in Marriage à la Mode or The Rake's Progress that is as laboured as this and as filled out to its corners. Because of this cold care An Election Entertainment might pass, for a moment, for a painting by Wilkie. It is, that is to say, almost a *pastiche* Hogarth. Perhaps it was because of this that Charles Lamb so much admired it, calling it a 'matchless' picture. Its composition consists of an oblong and an oval table, set side by side and touching each other, the thirty or forty figures being disposed in those patterns accordingly. Its character of the eighteenth century depends entirely upon the dress of the actors, for the setting is a plain undecorated room in a country inn. It is this, again, which relates An Election Entertainment to Wilkie.

Canvassing for Votes is, by contrast, the perfect embodiment of its time. A country inn, the Royal Oak, takes up the foreground of the picture. Its inn sign is covered with a painted election cloth, which is a little picture in itself. It shows a stream of money, or bribes, pouring out from the Treasury, which stands side by side with William Kent's Palladian building of the Horse Guards, then newly completed but in all essentials as it is now. Below this, the foreground of the election cloth shows Punch as a Candidate for Parliament, scattering money among the electors, who include a dreadful hunchback old dame in white cloak and apron and a black steeple hat. But the general purpose of the whole painting is to depict the various figures taking bribes from either, or both, sides in front of the inn. There are a bearded Jewish pedlar and a fat man, perhaps the publican,

39. LONDON STREET SCENE

40. THE MERRYMAKERS

The Rev. Matthew Peters

Royal Academy Diploma Gallery

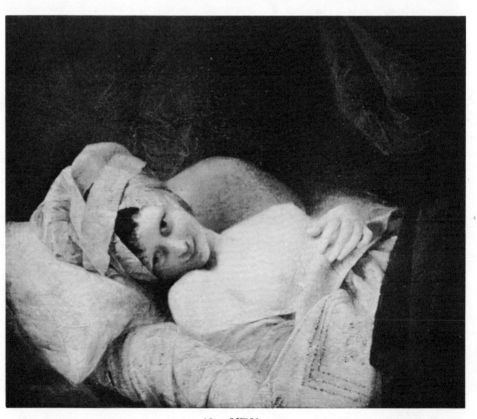

42. LYDIA

The Rev. Matthew Peters

The Earl of Granard

smoking his pipe in his shirt-sleeves, with his wig pushed up over his forehead. There is, also, in patriotic emblem, the wooden and gilded figurehead from a ship which stands outside the inn and has the form of a lion swallowing a *fleur-de-lys*. The Polling at the Hustings is not so successful as this. It is, indeed, the weakest painting in the series. The detail is lacking which usually lends an interest, if not an aesthetic one, to the majority of Hogarth's pictures. On the other hand, Chairing the Members redeems this series from bathos and is, in fact, an important and elaborate conception. The scene is, in arrangement, rather like a stage setting. It has a backcloth and two wings, that is to say, while the stage illusion is carried still further by the use Hogarth makes, once again, of a shadow. It is the shade of the defeated candidate, chaired by his supporters and being carried from the wings of the scene. This may be the last big composition by Hogarth. After it was finished his health began to fail, and he became involved in acrimonious disputes and wrangles which wasted his time. This is the last of his big series of paintings and, at this point, we can take our leave of him in order to take a view of painters who were contemporary with him.

CHAPTER III

EIGHTEENTH-CENTURY PAINTERS

THE necessity of devoting a separate chapter of this work to Hogarth must diminish, inevitably, the other primitives of our school of painters. It must, and it will be, some considerable time before there is an artist who can stand comparison with the inventor of Marriage à la Mode or The Rake's Progress. But the scope of this investigation must take us back earlier than Hogarth and, after that, to his contemporaries. It may not be too fanciful to find the foreshadowing of much that is to come in the drawing, by T. Johnson, of the Baths at Bath (44). Johnson, who worked in the manner of the Bohemian, Wenceslaus Hollar, gives a delightful rendering of the early architecture, that is so unlike the classical Bath. His figures, also, are excellent, having even a little of the touch of Cruikshank in them, particularly in the two men in black far away on the right-hand side of the drawing. Next to nothing is known of T. Johnson; but he may be regarded as, in some sense, the ancestor of Rowlandson or Cruikshank.

One of the very first of English painters, Francis Barlow, approaches, but never quite reaches, the limits we have set. He worked, tentatively, in too many directions, not content with the animal or sporting pictures that should have been his speciality, but painting ceilings as well, and designing, or so it is said, some of the monuments for Westminster Abbey. In fact he had ambitions, and the examples of Verrio and Laguerre led him to aspire into areas of which their, perhaps, greater incompetence was not afraid. We reproduce a typical, if not exceptional, drawing by Barlow, characteristic of his handling and of the subjects that he most often depicted (45). Barlow is a charming, if very minor, painter, and already in him there is something beginning to emerge which is neither French nor Flemish nor Italian.

The street scene by Gawen Hamilton, which provides our next illustration (39), is also, if charming, supremely unimportant as a work of art. Perhaps its ascription to Gawen Hamilton may be unconfirmed optimism, for this rare and unknown painter had a vigour in characterization which hardly emerges out of this placid scene. Yet, again, this is the beginning of the English scene. The dress of the young woman in the

43.   INTERIOR WITH FIGURES

J. M. Laroon

The Tate Gallery

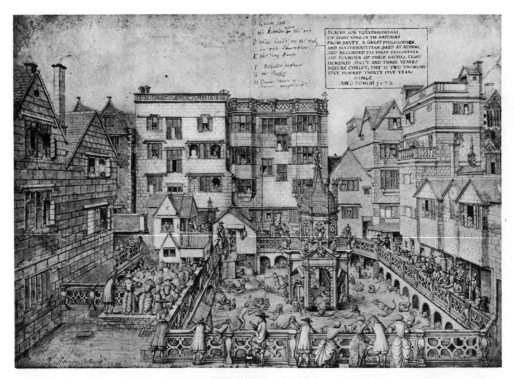

44.　THE BATHS AT BATH

T. Johnson

The British Museum

45.　A FARMYARD WITH FIGURES

Francis Barlow

The Victoria and Albert Museum

foreground is as English as the English figures in one of Canaletto's pictures of London; and his paintings of London are as different in costume as in architecture from his views of Venice. Also the house in this picture is the house, even now, of Cheyne Walk or of Stoke Newington. Its windows alone are characteristic of their time and place.

A Village School by Josef van Aken (47) is a delightful little painting without the sentimentality, or the tendency to caricature, which are inevitable from most pictures of a rural school. Van Aken, like Horremans, like Nollekens, like Rysbrack the sculptor, came from Antwerp. The foreigner may look in vain, at Antwerp, for works by this minor school of painters. Antwerp was a dying town then, and its energetic citizens emigrated abroad, particularly, for it was so near, to London. Van Aken and Horremans and Nollekens helped to found the English school of painting. It is probable, at least, that they took numerous pupils. These men, and the Dutchman Cornelius van Troost, are more nearly akin to our indigenous painting of the eighteenth century than any French or Italian artist of the time. Francis Hayman, a painter who was principally employed in making book illustrations and in the painted decorations for Vauxhall Gardens, illustrates the same tendencies (40). He is not quite distinguished enough in technique to be at once recognized in his pictures. There is a certain inherent weakness and deficiency, and then this comes to be known as the thing which is characteristic of Hayman. He is to be identified by his shortcomings and this will, perhaps, establish the small, if definite, measure that must be allowed to Hayman.

Marcellus Laroon is a person of altogether different stature. Nobody who has ever seen a Laroon could by any possibility fail to recognize his hand. It is one of the most strongly individual in the history of painting. Laroon was an amateur, but an amateur with the character of a Constantin Guys. We have drawn a comparison elsewhere between Laroon and George Cruikshank. Certain paintings by Laroon were known, at least, to Cruikshank, and in his illustrations to the eighteenth-century scene there are unmistakable signs that Cruikshank had profited from his lessons of Laroon. The mere strength of his personality, as expressed principally with his pen, conveys with it a curious assurance that this was how things really looked. This is the truth: and not the paintings of Watteau or Gainsborough. But, also, there is a natural affinity in technique between Marcellus Laroon and George Cruikshank. It goes further than this. There can be no doubt that, as personalities, they must have been in sympathy with one another. Laroon, it will be remembered, served through Marlborough's wars and through the Jacobite Rebellion of 1715. He was known to his contemporaries as Captain Laroon. A drawing that we have seen, dated 1707, shows a scene from one of his campaigns in Flanders. The soldier dancing, who is made to resemble a Mezzetin, is particularly well drawn. After the wars were over Laroon accompanied embassies to Ryswyck and to Venice. There are many doubts as to the chronology of his life. He seems to have retired from the army as late as 1734. At some time in his life Laroon was an actor. He was Harlequin in Rich's company. Because of this association Laroon had, like Cruikshank, a strong affinity with the theatre, which is proved in several beautiful drawings and at least one painting. It is known also that he gambled to excess. Laroon must have been in old age something of a legendary figure from the distant past. The writer has seen a drawing signed and dated 1772; drawn, that is to say, no less than sixty-five years after the scene that we have reproduced from Marlborough's wars. In this again he resembles Cruikshank, who was producing, to the astonishment of a few discerning persons, the last of his illustrations in the year 1875, some sixty-five years after he first became known, in the days of the Regency, as a caricaturist working in the manner of James Gillray. Laroon is so easily and quickly to be identified that it is curious his fame is not more widely spread. He is, as yet, scarcely represented in the public galleries, and it is probable that his paintings in considerable number may still await discovery.

A painter who is even less well known provides our next illustration. This is Peter Monamy, whose long life from 1670 till 1749 relates him to the reign of Charles II and puts his maturity in the reign of Queen Anne. He was born, it would seem, in Jersey, and coming to London was apprenticed to a house painter on old London Bridge. This painting, of the old East India Wharf at London Bridge (46), is probably the best of the marine subjects for which Monamy was famous in his day. If this was the scene that Monamy looked out upon during his early youth as apprentice there can be little wonder at its impelling him to become an artist. For this is a scene that would have a particular and compelling romance to any intelligent child. The giant forms of the Indian merchant-men loom up, with furled sails, through the mist. There are delightful passages in his rendering of the masts and rigging and an accuracy over these details of sea lore that may remind some persons of the marine pictures of Tissot, the painter of late Victorian life. The sailors are aloft among the ropes, and in the stillness of the air these sailing ships might be the glass ships under glass domes of the ideal curiosity shop, or, more still, the ideal and undisturbed drawing-room in which we may always hope to find them. Nearer at hand, in Monamy's picture, the unloading

46. THE OLD EAST INDIA WHARF AT LONDON BRIDGE

Peter Monamy

The Victoria and Albert Museum

47. A VILLAGE SCHOOL

J. Van Aken   Sir Edward Marsh

48. INTERIOR WITH FIGURES

W. Hodges

Joseph Wright of Derby   49. THE IRON FORGE   *Lord Mount Temple*

Joseph Wright of Derby   50. THE OLD MAN AND DEATH   *Mrs. K. M. Bright*

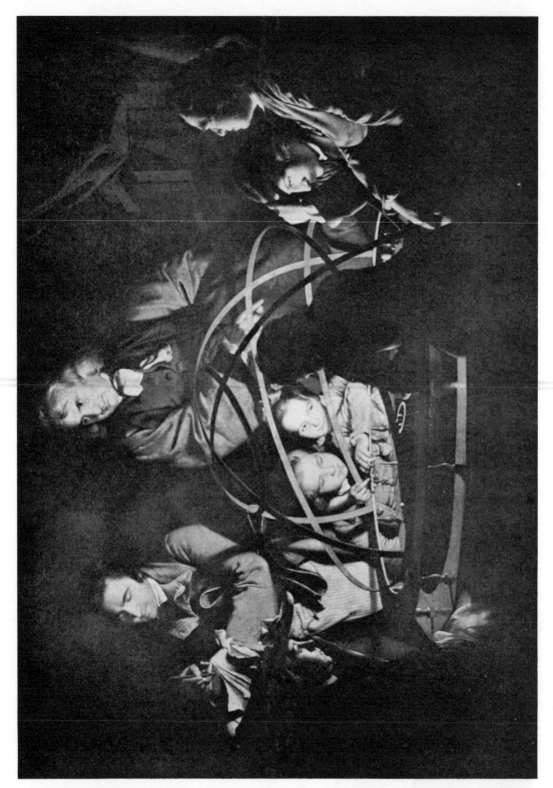

51. THE ORRERY

and checking of the cargo is taking place. There are huge barrels, perhaps of rum, and cases which can only contain tea, coffee or sugar. These are marked with mysterious cyphers which heighten the sense of mystery and romance attaching to bales and packages come from so distant a clime. But perhaps the charm of this picture by Monamy is in its reminder to us of the engraved headings upon old shop bills. The tea merchants, down till about 1850, had just such a scene as this reproduced in miniature for their headings, generally, though, with a touch of *chinoiserie* to add aroma to the choice Keemun or Mandarin of their stock.

We arrive, from this moment, into contact with greater names in painting. It will have been obvious, since Hogarth has received a separate treatment to himself, that Zoffany, who attained to perfection in the Conversation Piece, is the artist who might have been expected to succeed, just as fully, in the genre picture. It could, indeed, be argued that such paintings as the Tribuna of the Uffizi or the Towneley Marbles belong less to the Conversation Piece than they do to that school which is our present subject. They have transcended their own limits. Beginning, we might say, in the spirit of operetta, they are so fully expressed that they have become grand opera. Not that the ideal genre picture is by any necessity of heroic scale, but the fullest and most minute version of either Conversation Piece or genre picture reaches into a realm which is of neither, or is neutral to them both. Here, for an instance, is The Lapidaries, by Zoffany (5). This small painting, which hangs in the Royal collection at Windsor Castle, is a portrait of Peter Dollond, a famous optician of his time, and his assistant. They are in the workroom, as near as possible to the light of a window, in the act of grinding a lens. Mr. Dollond, an old man of about sixty-five, has his pair of spectacles pushed up on to the turban, or knotted handkerchief, that is bound round his head. This is because he has stopped his work for a moment in order to look straight at the artist. In another minute his glasses will come down on to his nose and he will resume his work. But this painting, in real truth, is no more than an excuse for the elaborate and painstaking rendering of numberless small objects—glass retorts, metal instruments with wooden handles, a steel saw, a pair of scissors, many small pots and bowls—all the tools and implements of his profession. It is a painting of still life; but, at the same time, in miniature, a portrait, a conversation piece, and a genre picture.

Our other painting by Zoffany, the Strolling Musicians (6), comes more strictly within our category. This, also, is a very small painting, and it is something peculiar and exceptional, without any parallel among his pictures. It was done on his Italian travels, during some transit to or fro

43

from Florence. He had been made a member of the Academy of Parma, perhaps on the strength of his portraits of the Habsburgs at Vienna, and this little picture was the diploma piece that he left behind him in the gallery at Parma. There it still hangs, not far from the great paintings of Correggio, the more striking, perhaps, because of its unexpectedness in those surroundings. But it is, at least, a curious anomaly, even as a Zoffany. The comic expression on the faces of the players is oddly German or Swiss in conception. The execution much resembles that of a Liotard. In fact, to those who know the late paintings in *gouache* by Liotard that are to be seen in the Rijksmuseum at Amsterdam, it is of Liotard, more than Zoffany, that we are reminded. Nevertheless, the known facts in connection with this picture establish it, beyond contradiction, as a work of Zoffany. But, in the body of his paintings, the Strolling Players of Parma must remain an exception and something of a contradiction.

After The Lapidaries and the Strolling Players there is an easy and chronological connection to those sort of paintings for which Wright of Derby is famous. They are pictures that must belong, beyond any doubt, to the same decade, at least, of years. They pose something of the same problems, and their invention and their handling are upon the same aesthetic level. The paintings by Wright of Derby are larger in size. They are important pictures and not isolated small experiments that occupy a place to themselves in the painter's output. But the measure of Zoffany, as against Wright of Derby, is expressed in this statement. Similar in merit to the small Lapidaries, these large paintings of The Orrery (51) or The Forge (49) are the masterpieces of Wright of Derby. They represented the best of which he was capable and, below them, he is painstaking but unexceptional. He began, in early life, by painting candlelight and firelight subjects which are difficult to know from those of 'Old' Morland, the father of George Morland. The Orrery, now in the Derby Museum, and the most famous work of his maturity, dates from 1765. The Orrery, a word which we can presume will be unknown in its implications to most of our readers, portrays a philosopher or scientist giving a lecture on the Orrery, and a lecture on that particular experiment in which a lamp is put in place of the sun. A group of persons, one lady and two boys, are gathered round this instrument, the Orrery, in order to watch the experiment. A hidden candle, in the middle of the group, throws its flickering light upon their faces and shadows the dark outlines of their clothes. All of these figures are said to be portraits, and the picture is certainly a fine and melodramatic thing with no trace of the amateur in its handling. Wright of Derby was one of the first of our provincial painters

44

52.   THE FRUITS OF EARLY INDUSTRY AND ECONOMY

George Morland   *McFadden Collection, Philadelphia*

53. THE COTTAGE DOOR

George Morland   *Royal Holloway College*

54. A VISIT TO THE BOARDING-SCHOOL

George Morland   *The Wallace Collection*

to achieve this status. He had succeeded in this by much labour, making copies, it is known, of Gerard Dou and of other Dutch artists who had specialized in those effects of artificial light in which he was interested.

Another painting by Wright of Derby, The Forge (49), now in the collection of Lord Mount Temple, is in some respects better as a picture than The Orrery. The figures are grouped in a tall room or smithy. Their attitudes are more dramatized and the characters more differentiated. There are women and children, as well as the two men at the forge and an old and patriarchal figure, who sits, watching, from the corner. Certainly the rendering of still life in this picture could not be bettered in respect of accurate representation. The barrel furnace, and the white-hot piece of metal that throws a blinding light upon everything round it, have the accuracy of a carefully posed photograph. It could not be more exact or correct as a painting. Because of this, it may be, The Forge has little importance as a work of art, but it shows, at least, other English painters, beside Hogarth, equipped after all this time for any project to which they are attracted. Wright of Derby has a competence which only Hogarth and Zoffany have, so far, possessed. Other pictures, beside The Orrery and The Forge, have this full display of his powers. The Experiment with the Air Pump is yet another painting of similar character. His historical pictures are far less interesting; his eruptions of Vesuvius are not convincing as scientific fact; his portraits are dull but supremely lifelike. So that this considerable painter may be seen in other moods than that upon which his fame depends, a picture of an old man with death approaching him as a skeleton is here reproduced (50). It shows Wright of Derby in an unfamiliar phase of his temperament; but The Orrery must ever remain his highest achievement and the picture for which he will be remembered. It is only necessary, in parenthesis, to compare its technique with the Interior by William Hodges, R.A. (48), in order to see the pre-eminence of Wright of Derby. Nevertheless, this Hodges was not without interest in his particular line. He accompanied, in the place of Zoffany who would not go at the last moment, Captain Cook in his second voyage round the world, drew the illustrations of South Sea Islands for his travels, and painted some large views of Tahiti for the Admiralty. Later in his life he lived for some considerable time in India.

But we come now to George Morland, who must remain, in his occasional strength and in his more frequent weaknesses, one of the most typical of English painters. So large is his output that it has been difficult to choose representative examples that are not hurried by his need to pay creditors, or made sentimental so that their natural charm is spoilt.

George Morland was the son and grandson of painters, and this inheritance is apparent in the ease and spontaneity of his composition. He would appear to have had no difficulty but his self-indulgence and weakness of character. This may be an easy reproach to make against any artist; but, in the case of Morland, it is, at least, justified in the known facts of his career. Some extraordinary stories are told of his intemperance, though it would seem that, as in the parallel cases of Toulouse-Lautrec and of Phil May, this accentuated, without injuring, his talent. Drink shortened his life, but it is not so easy to prove that it spoilt his genius. He was driven for want of money into ceaseless production. Had he not been an inveterate drunkard he would have painted far less. And the natural ease of his hand made it impossible for him to paint ungracefully. This anomalous situation is reached, therefore, that it was the vice of drink which drove Morland to paint so many pictures. Had he been innocent of this his output would have been much diminished and there is no reason to assume, knowing the spontaneous nature of his art, that his pictures would have been any the better for a more restrained exercise of his gift.

The engravings and mezzotints after George Morland, a great number of them being by his brother-in-law, William Ward, testify to the enormous fecundity of which we are speaking. Of his countless farmyard scenes, The Cottage Door (53), from the Royal Holloway College, is distinguished for its more careful treatment and finish. This painting is signed and dated 1790, so that it belongs to his best period. The characteristic looseness of its handling is most typical of Morland. It is an interesting comparison between this freedom of touch and the bold looseness of Fragonard in, for instance, one of his painted portrait heads. That, it will be apparent, in its derivation from Rembrandt and also from Tiepolo, is founded on the great tradition. Morland, on the other hand, whose powers were on much the same level as those of Fragonard, is nothing but English. A Lost Kite is another, most typical, Morland of the rustic kind. The wooden stile or fence in the picture could be nothing but the English scene; while the tree, again, in which the kite has become entangled, is something of a *tour de force*, to be compared, once more, with the trees of Fragonard. But Fragonard has a sense of poetry which is not to be found in Morland. He has sentiment but not poetry. The trees of Fragonard's *l'Escarpolette*, or of the *Foire de St. Cloud*, make Morland, by comparison, into a provincial and rustic painter.

But Morland exists also in another mood which confounds and contradicts this easy assumption. Where his grace is carried into less boorish surroundings he emerges as another Morland, quite different from

55. LADIES' RECREATIONS: NINEPINS

ohn Collet   *Viscount Bearsted*

56. THE PROMENADE AT CARLISLE HOUSE

the farmyard scene. A Visit to the Boarding School (54) is one of a pair of paintings, the other being A Visit to the Child at Nurse, of which coloured mezzotints were made by William Ward. These were painted in 1788-89, when Morland was twenty-six years old. The physical beauty of all the persons in the picture that we reproduce is to be commented upon. This is so strong a trait in Morland's painting that it amounts to a characteristic by which he is to be known and recognized. It is a legacy to us also from an age of exquisite taste and tact in all the appurtenances of life. This is the period of the late Adams, and of Henry Holland, the classical architect of the coming Regency. The dress of the little boy's mother, who is seated on the right-hand side of the picture, is the fashionable English dress of that period, which was the fashionable dress of the Continent. English fashions were the mode of that time, and the prints from this pair of pictures will have found their way into many foreign countries.

Another painting by Morland, The Fruits of Early Industry and Œconomy, in the McFadden collection at Philadelphia, is much more delightful than its sententious title might seem to suggest. The City merchant is sitting with his clerk or foreman at a window overlooking the river. His wharves, with bales of merchandise, are in full view. The parable of this picture lies in its happy contentment. The merchant's wife and family of small children, attended by a negro page, pose for their portraits in this room, which has for decoration a painting of their house in the country. The whole picture has an echo, which is even a little comical, of Hogarth. The ferocity of his satire has gone altogether; but, as though in emblem of that thing which Morland considered to be indispensable to human happiness, a fine mahogany wine-cooler, standing on the carpet, offers a flagon of whisky or sherry to all who come.

This class of picture by Morland with which we have been dealing, which was painted, as it were, almost expressly in order to be engraved, includes, also, many paintings by other men of so similar a type that they form a school, almost, and no better title could be found, perhaps, than the Mezzotint School as a name by which to denote these paintings of daily sentiment. Francis Wheatley is an artist who comes to mind at once in this connection. This very considerable painter has suffered to his detriment from the over-popularity of his Cries of London. As in the case of Rachmaninov, whose Prelude in F minor has never been forgiven to him, Wheatley exists for most people only as the painter of those sentimentalized scenes which must have been so far from the daily truth in this metropolis of slums. Few people have had the curiosity to enquire further of Wheatley than his Cries of London. But he was, for instance,

47

an excellent architectural draughtsman. He lived for some years in Dublin and, apart from the work of James Malton, to which we shall refer later on, that supreme example of Georgian town architecture has no better memorial than the tinted drawing by Wheatley, still to be seen in Dublin, of the Speaker of the Irish House of Commons entering in state with his officers into the Parliament Building. But Wheatley, as a painter, had many directions of activity. He painted small portraits and was even engaged on the decorations of Vauxhall Gardens. A universal competence, equal to that of Morland, and a beautiful touch make of him, after Gainsborough, one of the best of our native painters. A series of four pictures, Maidenhood, Courtship, Marriage, and Married Life (58-61) are typical of this painter in their suaveness and physical beauty. It is to be felt of Wheatley, as it is of Gainsborough or of Morland, that they must have been themselves of a handsome presence in order to achieve this contented, effortless ease and grace. Perhaps they were too charming, as persons, to be great painters.

It is significant, when dealing with what we have termed the Mezzotint School, that one of the most lovely of English eighteenth-century drawings should be the Promenade at Carlisle House (56), drawn in coloured crayons by the great engraver John Raphael Smith. How different this is from the *gouaches* of the French *petits maîtres*, from Lavreince and Baudouin and Boilly! In their works, which are always exquisite in finish, the figures are in animated conversation. They are dressed with impeccable taste in the last word of fashion. Here, in the hands of John Raphael Smith, this interior of a well-known gambling house presents to us a scene which is different in all details. The foreground is taken up by two young women who are of a ravishing prettiness, but as silent as the figurants in an old musical comedy at Daly's or the Gaiety. The shades of Miss Lily Elsie and Miss Evelyn Laye look at us out of this drawing. The two young women are dressed in the English mode of the time, which owed nothing to French fashions. On the contrary these were the English clothes that were copied on the Continent, while English gardens were laid out and English mezzo-tints were collected. The man who leans on his walking-stick and looks so closely at the two young women may be the artist himself; while, certainly, these two are portraits. This drawing gives us the physical truth of the fashionable, or half-fashionable, world. Nobody in life was really like the figures in Wheatley's Cries of London. Here, on the contrary, these are two authentic young women, and of a nationality that could not be mistaken. There is a glorious, an almost exaggerated sanity about this drawing. It is so much less fussy and pernickety than a Zoffany, for the figures really move and breathe against their background and are not

Francis Wheatley

57.   A HOLIDAY RESORT WITH GIPSIES

Lord Brocket

Francis Wheatley   59.   COURTSHIP   *Viscount Bearsted*

Francis Wheatley   58.   MAIDENHOOD   *Viscount Bearsted*

Francis Wheatley   Viscount Bearsted

60   MARRIAGE

61.   MARRIED LIFE

Francis Wheatley   Viscount Bearsted

63. MARRIAGE

By Courtesy of the Knoedler Galleries   W. Williams

62. COURTSHIP

W. Williams   By Courtesy of the Knoedler Galleries

isolated in it in dumb action as upon the stage. Unfortunately little or nothing more of the original work of John Raphael Smith can be traced. He 'scraped,' to use the curious term of the old dictionaries of painting, some hundred and fifty mezzotints; he drew a few small portraits in crayons, but of his original drawings this may well be the most important that he executed. John Raphael Smith is, in fact, like so many of the English painters, an artist *manqué*. The same society which induced Gainsborough to renounce landscape for portrait painting kept John Raphael Smith at making mezzotints from the portraits painted by other men when he should have been using his exquisite touch upon his own conceptions.

Belonging to this same school as Wheatley or as John Raphael Smith is another painter, Henry Walton, who is a better artist than either of them. This rarest of English painters, for his authentic works can almost be counted on the fingers of one hand, is known to many by his painting, in the National Gallery, of a woman plucking a fowl. For some time this picture was attributed to Chardin, for it has a superficial resemblance to Chardin, though the handling is lighter and less serious. One of the most famous of English mezzotints is by John Raphael Smith after Walton. The subject of this is The Cherry Barrow; but the oil painting from which the print is taken (64) may be the most lovely English painting of the eighteenth century. The writer has known this picture since early childhood and, as a work of art, it has lasted for him all his lifetime. It would be difficult to indicate for those who have not seen it in what the curious and exceptional quality of this painting is to be found. No other name has any connection or resemblance to it, except in the case of Goya, who, in his portraits done before the end of the eighteenth century, could invest the clothes in a portrait with this intense and luminous transparency of colour. His portrait of the Condesa de Chinchon, shown in the centenary exhibition of his works in Madrid in 1928, had this quality which it is so hard to describe. Also, the plain background of the Walton picture, formed by the receding line of the wall, has something of Goya, just as the children round the cherry barrow have a reminiscence of Murillo. It must be remembered that Henry Walton, who was a connoisseur of painting and one of the first restorers of old masters, has put forth all his taste and discrimination in this masterpiece from his hand. The hint of Murillo, therefore, is not to be mistaken. It is equivalent to a classical allusion in poetry. The dress upon which such delicate care has been lavished is a hooped skirt of an indescribable rose colour, or it is a transparent and filmy white worn over the rose. It is supposed to be the artist's wife who is portrayed. Her arms are also most beautifully painted, as are her hands.

She wears a high fur hat, shaped like a Guardsman's bearskin, and which imparts a solemn gravity to her and gives the composition its hieratic importance. Her fur cap is the apex of the triangle upon which the group of figures is planned. The little girl, who is the painter's daughter, is a typically beautiful English child wearing an enchanting hat, which is decorated with a pale-blue silk ribbon, in the same key, so to speak, as the pink of her mother's dress. The old woman who is selling the cherries is the least important part of the drama. All the rest of its interest lies in the children who are buying from the barrow. The London oyster-shell sky rises up in the background, above the dark and smoky houses. There is a tradition in the writer's family that this same wall which provides the background for the painting was, or still is, in existence somewhere in Spitalfields or that region of London. The painter, Henry Walton, who was an amateur, was a friend of the family. They owned at one time another picture by him, a portrait of a bookseller at York who was a well-known character in his time. Of other paintings by Walton as fine as The Cherry Barrow there would seem only to be the picture known as Miss Curtis, or The Muff. This is familiar from the mezzotint made after it. It shows a beautiful young woman sitting on a sofa. She is wearing a large hat and a fur muff. There is no indication as to the colour of her dress, which might be of a rich and deep dark red. This painting is known to be still in existence; and on the strength of these two paintings alone, The Cherry Barrow and Miss Curtis, Henry Walton deserves a fame perhaps only less in degree than that which has never been denied, whatever the vagaries of taste, to Gainsborough. Fortunately another painting by Walton, the Pretty Maid buying a Love Song (65), in the collection of Lord Mildmay of Flete, will serve as an illustration of his genius. The subjects that he chose to paint are as simple and diurnal as those of the Dutch artists. For its incident, or story, this picture might be a Nicholas Maes, or a de Hoogh; but, in the physical sense, this could never be the work of a Dutchman. The figure of the servant girl is absolutely characteristic of this painter. It is an unmistakable Walton, and in its pose has a marked resemblance to the figure of the painter's wife in The Cherry Barrow. She is posed, that is to say, against an almost similar background, part, it may be, of the same wall that appears in the other painting. The ballad seller is curious because of his little identity with the eighteenth century. He is in the clothes of a later century and has the face and appearance of an actor. Altogether, this picture, like The Cherry Barrow, has an especial appeal because of its hintings at a school of London paintings which never went further than these beginnings, but is as typical of London,

64. THE CHERRY SELLER

Henry Walton

Captain Osbert Sitwell

65. A PRETTY MAID BUYING A LOVE SONG

Henry Walton

Lord Mildmay of Fleet

in an elegance and beauty all its own, as the works of the French *petits maîtres*, Lavreince, Baudouin, Debucourt, are typical of Paris. That might have been the importance of Henry Walton's art; in default of it we are left with two or three paintings, one of which, at any rate, is as lovely as anything that can be found in English painting of the eighteenth century.

That this school was more than a distant possibility can be proved in the work of other painters. The Poultry Seller (80), by a completely unknown artist, Richard Heighway, could be described as a weak Walton, for it is certainly in his manner. There were, also, minor George Morlands, who produced endless subjects for the engravers. Two titles, taken at random, At the Inn Door and Courtship, are typical of innumerable soothing or sentimental subjects that were afterwards reproduced in mezzotint. Many of these prints, which are by world-famous engravers, may be supposed to be better than the original paintings from which they were taken. This is not the case with The Cherry Barrow; that is the measure of Walton. With Henry Singleton it is a very different matter. The engravers had become more finished artists than the painters who worked for them, and this, in due course, was the symptom of decline. Singleton and Heighway are tag-ends of the century. Nothing more was to be expected of it in this direction.

It is time, in fact, to turn our attention to the smaller things. If, in the case of at least one artist who is to be mentioned, he can be placed on the strength of his drawings among the greater personalities of the eighteenth century, this must be the measure of an age of decay, which had begun from the top and had not affected yet the lower extremities of life. The fine simplicities of late Adam design are contemporary with such charming minor things as the drawing that we reproduce by James Malton (66). Its subject is a street in Dublin; and it is one of the series from which perhaps the finest aquatint book of the eighteenth century was compiled. Malton, as an architectural draughtsman, had been a pupil of Paul Sandby, who, in his turn, had been the ardent disciple of Canaletto. This chain of associations will explain the peculiar excellence of Malton's drawing. It is Capel Street, Dublin, with a direct view of a bridge over the Liffey, ending with the Royal Exchange in the distance. The bow-windows and fanlights of the old State Lottery Office are shown on the left of the drawing, beyond which can be seen the masts and rigging of a ship close up against the Georgian façades on the other side of the river. But the figures with which his drawings are enlivened are not the least part of Malton's work. Two ladies on the left, who are passing by the windows of the Lottery Office, might be stepping from the pages of

Heideloff's *Gallery of Fashion*. Moreover, this drawing is not by any means the best out of the book in which it appears. There are quite half a dozen plates to which this is inferior. It is, we may add in parentheses, a wonderful achievement in plain aquatint; but, if this book can be seen in its rarer, coloured state, the *Architectural Views of Dublin* by James Malton will stay in the memory as the supreme rendering of a Georgian town. After this, a look at London as it is to remain under our new Georgian epoch is enough to wring pity from a heart of stone.

After the drawing by Malton we place a view of the Pump Room at Bath by Humphrey Repton (67). The *clou* of this is the two beaux who are trying to attract the attention of a young woman standing at the counter. These three figures are as full of character as in a drawing by Debucourt. The remainder of the drawing lapses too much into Bunbury-like caricature, but it is interesting as being the work of such a versatile man as Repton. He was then over thirty years of age, but had not yet begun his career as landscape architect and gardener. In that, together with Nash, with whom he was often associated, Repton became one of the most important men of the late eighteenth century and the Regency. Not only was he the leading landscape gardener after Capability Brown, but he seems to have been responsible, in the first place before Nash, for Brighton Pavilion. He was convinced, after working at that curious house Sezincote, in Gloucestershire, that 'architecture and gardening were on the eve of some great future change, in consequence of our having lately become acquainted with the scenery and buildings in the inner provinces of India.' This change, which he foreshadowed in his designs at Sezincote, found its only other expression in Brighton Pavilion; but Repton, whose drawing shows the environment into which he was born, contrived to effect great and considerable changes in visual life. This was due in large part to his skill as a draughtsman and to the fine drawings with which his books were illustrated. It is probable, though, that this view of the Pump Room at Bath is a unique instance of Repton working in the manner of Rowlandson.

That conjunction of names is made the easier by transition through the odd works of Robert Dighton. His drawing, Men of War bound for a Port of Pleasure (71), is an agreeable performance in a minor key. The Westminster Election (70) is much more elaborately finished and studied. Covent Garden is the scene, and turning back from this to The Four Times of Day: Morning, we see the passage of a generation across the scene. Tom King's Coffee-house, which is familiar to us from that shivering, frozen dawn, seems to have disappeared from in front of the church; but this is the exact scene as preserved for us, also, in one or two of the plates

James Malton

66. CAPEL STREET, DUBLIN

The Victoria and Albert Museum

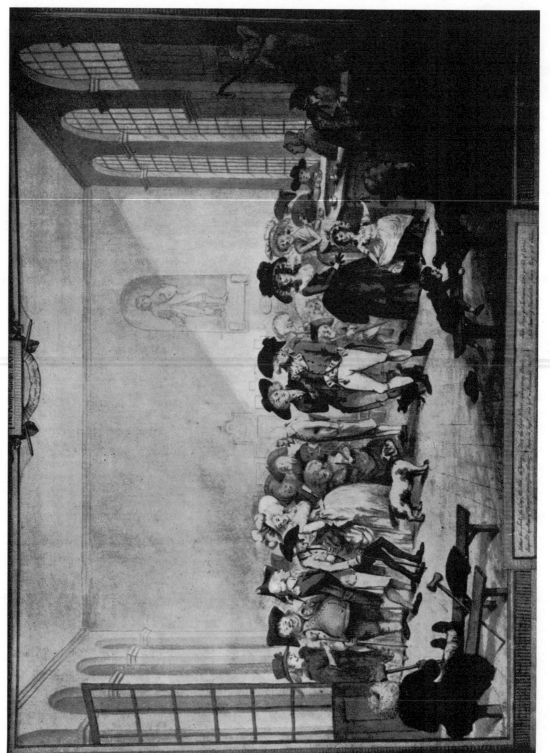

67. THE PUMP ROOM AT BATH

Samuel Collings

68. FROST ON THE THAMES

Dr. L. C. Parkes

69. A TRIP TO SCARBOROUGH

C. Bretherton

The Marquess of Lansdown

70. THE WESTMINSTER ELECTION

Robert Dighton

Ralph Edwards, Esq.

71.   MEN OF WAR BOUND FOR THE PORT OF PLEASURE

Robert Dighton

The British Museum

72. THE REAPERS

George Stubbs   *Viscount Bearsted*

73. THE HAYMAKERS

George Stubbs   *Viscount Bearsted*

74. VIEW IN HEREFORDSHIRE: HARVEST

G. R. Lewis

The Tate Gallery

75. THE HARVEST WAGGON

Thomas Gainsborough

Lord Swaythling

76. TREPANNING A RECRUIT

W. R. Bigg   *The Russell-Cotes Art Gallery, Bournemouth*

77. THE WOUNDED SOLDIER

James Ward   *J. J. Tufnell, Esq.*

78. "DRAWING TAUGHT"

E. F. Burney

E. F. Burney

79.   AN ELEGANT ESTABLISHMENT FOR YOUNG LADIES

The Victoria and Albert Museum

81. GIRL AT THE WATERFALL.   D. Maclise

The Victoria and Albert Museum

80. THE POULTRY SELLER   Attributed to R. Heighway

The Victoria and Albert Museum

P. J. De Loutherbourg

82.   A MIDSUMMER'S AFTERNOON WITH A METHODIST PREACHER

The National Gallery of Canada, Ottawa

from Cruikshank's *Comic Almanack* in the 'thirties of the nineteenth century, fifty years ahead of this. We see Covent Garden through Hogarth and Dighton and Cruikshank three times during a century, and now, another hundred years later, even the demolition of most of the houses in the background has not been able to alter the essential character of what we see. The two tall women in the English fashion of the seventeen-eighties, as also the woman in the large hat driving in the gig, impart the nationality of this scene just as surely as it is conveyed in the Cockney crowd, in Hawksmoor's portico of the church, or in the Georgian houses backing on the Strand. Ladies' Recreations (55), by the unknown John Collett, is a picture of ladies drinking and playing ninepins, and here again the nationality could be nothing but English. The same remark can be applied also to the two little paintings by W. Williams (62, 63).

The Harvest Waggon, by Gainsborough (75), is perhaps as near as that most graceful of our painters ever attained to the genre picture. How typical of Gainsborough are the trees, and also the figure of the boy who holds back the horses' heads. Two pastoral pictures by George Stubbs (72, 73) reveal that painter of sporting pictures in a mood which may be unfamiliar to some readers. The Reapers, especially, is a beautiful and tranquil painting of rural England. A Harvest Scene in Herefordshire, by G. R. Lewis (74), connects itself with the two pictures just mentioned. A contrast can be made between this and the Frozen Thames by Samuel Collings (68). Francis Wheatley can be exhibited in a charming drawing of a gipsy encampment (57); while the painting of a Methodist preacher making his sermon on Midsummer afternoon (82) is a grotesque, or caricature, landscape. Loutherbourg, one of the earliest of English water-colour painters, was a considerable artist in his way. This may be the only appearance of the Methodists in art.

But the end of this chapter must be devoted to a curious, minor draughtsman with a manner that was all his own. E. F. Burney, who lived to an immense age, dying as late as 1844, was the nephew of Fanny Burney. Drawing Taught (78) is a kind of graphic pun on the word 'drawing.' It will be more interesting to let it speak for itself. An Elegant Establishment for Young Ladies is more elaborate. A Fuseli-like figure may be noted on the left, sitting with her back to the spectator. Burney, who did some delightful small decorations for books and almanacs, is an almost for-gotten man, and may never in his day have achieved more than an amateur renown. He is, in fact, delightfully unimportant and, because of that, the more pleasant as a private possession. For that, in effect, is the pleasure that is derived from such minor discoveries.

CHAPTER IV

NINETEENTH-CENTURY PAINTERS

THE painters of anecdote and incident are to take on new directions and exploit new possibilities of their art in the nineteenth century. And yet, before 1820 and after 1860, the painting of such pictures has become nearly non-existent. It was to flourish exceedingly for those forty years and no more, a period which coincides with the greatest epoch of our material prosperity. The Crimean War and, still more, the Indian Mutiny were in the nature of nasty shocks to our national susceptibility. And, after that, the cloud of dullness descended, only to be broken by the jejune and disastrous 'nineties, in which time the only real artist, it is apparent, was Aubrey Beardsley. The reign of George IV, due to that monarch in greater part than is generally recognized, is a period of major importance in our art and letters, while the particular art that is under discussion in these pages had the closest association, and was the parallel or corollary to letters. The reign of George IV was the period of Sir Thomas Lawrence, of Turner and of Constable, of Bonington, Crome and Cotman. It was the time, also, of Byron, Keats, and Shelley, of Coleridge, of Jane Austen, and of Sir Walter Scott. One of the greatest epochs of the printed book was now in progress, for the art of aquatint illustration has never, before or since, reached such a pitch of excellence. The English coloured-plate books are the highest achievement of the time in contemporary Europe. There were, as well, considerable architects, of whom John Nash and J. B. Papworth were the most eminent. A wealth of Regency town houses, in circles and crescents, in squares and parades and terraces, are the works of these architects and their lesser satellites. These things, which are common knowledge, need only to be mentioned in order to remind ourselves that the maligned Prince Regent does really occupy, in spite of obloquy and adverse criticism, something of that position which he would have chosen for himself as a patron of art. The years succeeding the Battle of Waterloo showed the British people in an enviable advantage over their continental neighbours. England, alone, of European countries had painters, authors, poets, architects. This was only to last for a very few years, but for a time it was the incontrovertible truth. Only the Russia of Alexander I and his

83. PUNCH, OR MAY DAY

B. R. Haydon

The Tate Gallery

brother Nicholas I, the St. Petersburg of Pushkin and of the classical architects, Quarenghi and Rossi, was any rival to London. But St. Petersburg was at the end of Europe. London was its flourishing centre.

And yet this age was the time of conscious revival. The novels of Sir Walter Scott, *The Ancient Mariner*, *La Belle Dame Sans Merci*, the historical subjects of Bonington, the classical colonnades of the new Regent Street, what are these but conscious and closely considered archaisms? The Romantic Movement, in large part the invention of Englishmen, was spreading all through Europe. This, which has been one of the most sustained imaginative feats of the European mind, is still too near to us to be seen in all its immense entirety. It is a movement that, in its scope, was as far-reaching as the Renaissance; as the decadence of that into the Baroque or Rococo; or as the entire classical revival in Europe, with its poets, painters, architects, and sculptors. This movement, which may have begun with the supposed poems of Ossian and of Thomas Chatterton, with Goethe's *Werther*, was to influence the art of every European nation for a century to come. If it was to inspire the works of literature that will occur, at once, to mind, its effects were not less tremendous in every direction into which we can enquire. Its successive waves, or phases, gave us such diverse things as the Gothick of Walpole; the Windsor of Wyattville; the Byronic poems of Pushkin; Mickiewitz, whose poems inspired Chopin; the entirety of our own Pre-Raphaelite movement, including its true genius, Swinburne; the music of Weber, and much of the music of Schubert and Schumann. It inspired, as well, all the operas of Verdi, whose relation, indeed, to romantic opera is that of Sir Walter Scott to the Romantic novel. Its supreme masterpiece in music is, it is probable, the *Faust* symphony of Liszt; while the romanticism is not less potent in the wonderful *Romeo and Juliet* overture of Tchaikowsky, in his tone poem, *Francesca da Rimini*, and in the *Manfred* symphony, written as late as 1886, but still to be included as one of the greatest works of the Romantic revival. These works of Tchaikowsky are in its Byronic, not its Pre-Raphaelite mood; but, if these two divisions of its temperament mark the two best known of its manifestations, there are, as well, many curious undercurrents, of which the importance is more far-reaching than their visible presence might suggest.

This will mean the revival of forgotten names. In the history of art there are painters, in thinking of whom it is necessary to mention El Greco, or Blake, or Cézanne, whose influence after their own deaths becomes altogether exaggerated in proportion to the amount of recognition they received in their own lifetimes. But there are as well, in every branch of art, the artists who fail in their material careers but are assimilated, as it were unconsciously, into the whole blood-stream of the future generation. They are, in some sense, the precursors of the future; but, once absorbed into that, they still fail of recognition. There is another phenomenon as well, that of the personality who achieved ample rewards in his lifetime but is now disproportionately forgotten. The effects, for instance, of the Romantic tone poems of Tchaikowsky have passed into the accepted language of dramatic effects. Their whirling, clashing excitement belongs to that category to which such poems of Swinburne as the unique and lovely 'Anactoria' may be said to pertain. They are as closely related in their canon of art as Tennyson's 'Lady of Shalott' stands to the Pre-Raphaelite pictures of Millais or of Arthur Hughes. Their connection and relationship are too close to be ignored. But we shall find works of the Romantic Age, dating from not less than a century before this, which fulfil all the necessary conditions and are part and parcel of the movement. It is necessary, in fact, in this chapter which deals with some painters of the nineteenth century, to include works which were executed as early as the seventeen-eighties. And it will be found, in the particular instance of which we are thinking, that the paintings or drawings in question might be dated with impunity at any time for another forty years after the actual time of their creation.

The painter, then, with whom this chapter must open is the nearly forgotten Fuseli. Henry Füssli, or Fuessly, was born at Zürich in 1741, a member of a numerous family of painters, good, bad, and indifferent. He was, perhaps, a typical German Romantic and his early years were devoted to various attempts in different forms of literature. Fuseli came to London in 1767 and, encouraged by Sir Joshua Reynolds, decided on the career of a painter and went to Italy to study, where he remained for nine years. It was during this time in Rome that he met with the Edinburgh painter, John Brown, an altogether forgotten personality who had the consumption and, as well, some of the peculiar talent of Aubrey Beardsley. Fuseli must have been powerfully influenced by John Brown. The few drawings by Brown, which are nearly all that is left of him, might be signed by Fuseli, so close is their similarity. He died at thirty-five years of age and seems to have been altogether unnoticed by criticism until the last few years. In Edinburgh he worked in association with the historical painter, Alexander Runciman, whose chief work was a series of frescoes from Ossian. Here, also, are the beginnings of Romanticism. The frescoes in question were destroyed by fire about thirty years ago. Little is known about Runciman and, in fact, both Alexander Runciman and John Brown

84. THE NIGHTMARE

Henry Fuseli

Professor Ganz

85.　THE DEMOLITION OF THE DOMINICAN CHAPEL AT GENOA

Sir Thomas Lawrence

Duc de Trévise

deserve a detailed study, for their deaths in, respectively, 1785 and 1787 relate them to the very first phase of the Romantic movement. It can be said, however, that their work is continued in the long and varied career of Fuseli.

During his nine years in Rome it is easy to say that Fuseli fell under the influence of Michelangelo. The Rome of Bernini and Borromini, it is certain, had no effect upon him at all. Nine years is a long period out of a young man's life, and Fuseli seems to have had little to show for it. Much of the time may have been wasted in discussion, for Fuseli was a person in whom accomplishment always fell short of promise. Also, he was too near to literature to feel altogether happy in painting. There is ample evidence, though, that he studied painting, for Fuseli was a great connoisseur and was in later years to edit a dictionary of painters which does credit to his taste and erudition. Its extravagances of phrase are an amusing parallel to everything that is known of Fuseli in his life and in his work, and there are many turns of language which betray the oddity and strangeness of his temperament. Fuseli is always quoted as the disciple of Michelangelo. It would seem, though, more likely, in an extreme case such as his own, that Fuseli liked to write about painting and to paint about literature. There is more of the influence of the poet and dramatist Alfieri in Fuseli's paintings and drawings than there is tangible proof of his study of Michelangelo. Alfieri had the temperament which would exactly appeal to Fuseli. His shock of wild, red hair; his team of white horses with which he travelled even to Norway; his liaison, romantic in idea if not in fact, with the wife of the Young Pretender, all these traits of his life make Alfieri the translation into energy of the musings of Fuseli.

Soon after his return to London, in 1782, Fuseli produced his once famous and most characteristic work, The Nightmare (84). This picture, as we have said at an earlier page in this book, might well be taken from *Melmoth the Wanderer*, the Romantic novel by the Dublin clergyman, Maturin, which was published forty years later, in 1822. Fuseli, it would seem, then, was not a precursor in painting but a prophet, in painting, of what was to be the direction of certain forms of literature in the next generation after his own. The Nightmare, perhaps, is Fuseli's nearest approach to a good picture; or, if this is not his masterpiece, that name can be given to Mrs. Siddons as Lady Macbeth, a painting which is wonderfully weird and dramatic in conception. At about this time Fuseli painted several pictures for Boydell's *Shakespeare Gallery* and later, in 1799, opened his own Milton Gallery, which, as we have seen, consisted of nearly fifty pictures by his hand. It is only necessary to add that he was, later, made keeper and lecturer on painting at the Royal Academy and lived to an extreme old age, dying in 1825.

This strange character, who was poised between literature and painting, who was more interested to write of painting, and to paint when under the inspiration of poetry, never attained quite the technical skill that would have enabled him to realize his visions. He was of wilful and utmost eccentricity, pushing every aid of temperament and personality to their extremes in order to assert himself and attain justice to his talent. The legend that he ate raw meat before sleeping in order to induce nightmares may be dismissed as too facile, but there is no doubt that he was the true product of an age which loved the *Tales of Terror*. The supernatural was his especial *forte*, and it is sad to think that he only missed, by a hundred years, the discovery of the subconscious. As it is, he hovered many times on the borders of that. Given his trend of temperament, it would be easy to guess that the drawings by Fuseli are nearer to his intention than his large oil paintings.

The drawings by his hand are very numerous and vary widely in style. There are many drawings by him which are no better than weak Flaxmans. They lack the correct draughtsmanship and the cameo purity of Flaxman. There are, as well, the drawings by Fuseli which show the mutual influences between himself and William Blake. This, again, is a subject which has never yet received adequate study. None of the authorities upon William Blake have had the patience thoroughly to sift the evidence of Fuseli's paintings and drawings. In the absence of that knowledge it is impossible to determine the exact relation to each other of these two different sorts of visionaries, who, on occasion, approached so near to each other. The engravings by Blake for Young's *Night Thoughts*, as, again, for his edition of Blair's *Grave*, are very near in spirit to Fuseli. Spectral or nightmare subjects form another division of Fuseli's drawings. These are often to be distinguished by a figure in plated armour. Then, there are the drawings or sketches from purely literary subjects; and another series in which the figure of a charlatan or mountebank appears, in whom a direct influence can be traced from Alessandro Magnasco. It is obvious that Fuseli must have seen, while in Italy, some of the paintings of this other genius of the eccentric.

But, of all Fuseli's work, his highest accomplishment lies in various drawings done, it would seem, at different periods of his life in illustration of nothing in particular. They are co-ordinated, almost into a series of works, by certain characteristics that they have in common. They are dreams, or visions, or states of mind; but seen in terms of close, of day-to-day realism. They have a strange intensity of unimportance, a sort of trance-like focus, that dwells hypnotically upon such subjects as the figure of a woman standing by a fireplace, or dressing in front of a mirror. These ordinary things have become sinister and extraordinary. They are transcendental studies of the commonplace; but always in association with subjects which have an esoteric and, it may be, an erotic interpretation to be given to them. Also, the improbable details of the dream consciousness appear in them, unexplained and without reason. It is this which makes these drawings weird and unexpected. For these details are given without comment and with as great a degree of realism as the commonplaces, the chairs or tables of the scene.

Two of these drawings, in particular, may claim our attention. The first is a study of a female figure standing by a mantelpiece. She is dressed in the long, clinging garments that were the fashion at the time, but is transported into the nightmare world by the curious expression of her features which have that sort of intensified or spectral horror which is unaccountable, which transcends reality, and which is only encountered in the mazes of the subconscious world. Those are the true realms of Pluto, more realistically horrible than the *diableries* of the mediaeval imagination. In what these effects consist it is nearly impossible to say. Crouching at the feet of this figure are the forms of two more women, drawn in a convention which shows that they are in normal proportion, and are not dwarfs or stunted children, although their height is only about a third of that of the standing figure. At the same time it is to be observed that her height has nothing gigantic about it. Therefore, the effect given by this drawing is that the imagination of the artist worked separately upon this sheet of paper and conceived of the subject in two entirely unrelated dimensions. The one world in this drawing is, it may be, unaware of the other; or they dwell together in the same natural harmony as that of the world which shelters the insect feeding on the green blades of the grass and the giant forms of the cattle grazing on the same field and sustained by the same nourishment.

The other drawing (7) is, in all probability, the masterpiece of Fuseli. It represents a woman standing at her dressing-table, but these mere words can convey but little of its flourish of importance, or of the esoteric nature of its details. This is, however, a drawing which can be reproduced with remarkable success, so that some idea of its peculiar quality is conveyed in the illustration. It is to be remarked, at once, that this drawing is pure Fuseli; it is not the Fuseli who is half Flaxman, or a sad imitation of the Italian. This is a large, bold work done, so to speak, without fear of the technical consequences. The forms of the figures have some suggestion of the praying mantis about them, that feminine insect which, after preening itself, affects a kneeling or praying posture and kills and devours its companion. It would be ridiculous to suggest that the praying mantis was in the mind of Fuseli when he made this drawing, but it has a spiritual or a subconscious analogy to that atavistic world in which such impossibilities become fact and are the universal rule. Moreover, there are details in this drawing which quite defy explanation. It is interesting to glance, first of all, at the fine sweep of the ostrich plumes, and at the objects upon the dressing-table set out in meticulous array and drawn with convincing realism and probability. For the armoured-looking attendant, who is helping to dress the lady, wears on her head something which it is impossible to determine with accuracy but which might be a piece of plated armour, a sleeve or steel gorglet, or some brass or copper utensil of kitchen or fireplace. They might be armoured matadors putting the last touches to their defences before engaging in the tauromachic fight. Such shocks of incongruity or improbability as this drawing will impart are of a description to which it is most difficult to find a parallel. They are the incoherences of Hieronymus Bosch, or of the over-self-conscious Surrealist painters. But drawings by Fuseli, such as that we are discussing, must have been done entirely for his own pleasure and, unlike the Surrealists, without any aim at shocking the public. It is probable that they were hidden for years on end in his portfolios, only emerging in order to be shown to a restricted circle of friends. There are other drawings by Fuseli, still more extreme in nature, of which this must certainly be true. In these he seems to have found a fascination in the contrast between nude figures and their carefully dressed hair, elaborated in the extremes of fashion. Their curled and scented locks, dressed like the heads of antique gems or statues, seen through the contemporary modes of the Directoire, give the themes of these intensely erotic works. But, for that reason, they are more obvious and that much the less interesting than such a superb drawing as The Toilet. For, on the strength of this one work alone, Fuseli can occupy an exceptional place among draughtsmen.

And its exceptional or transcendental features, drawn, we must think, from the subconscious, may bring for Fuseli in the not-distant future a fame which has been denied to him for more than a hundred years. His works need to be carefully sifted before they are rejected. He painted much fustian and pure nonsense, but also some most interesting things which deserve to be carried back once more into the light. Many of his paintings must be in the attics and lumber-rooms of country houses. It

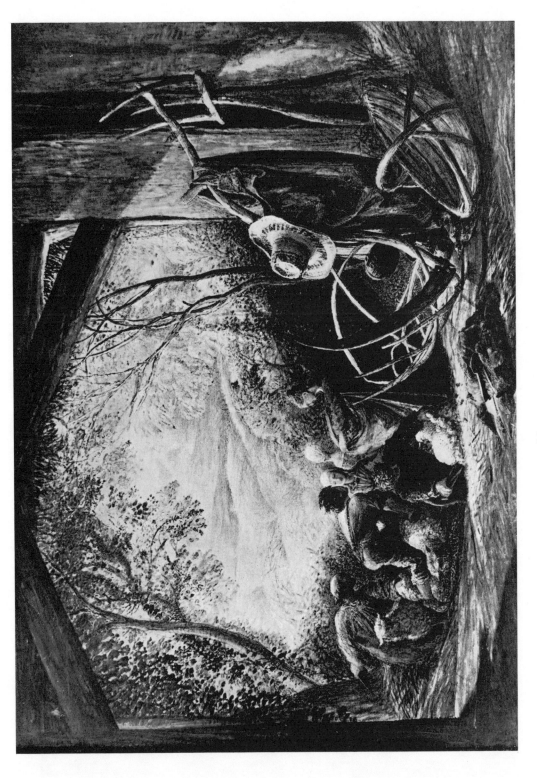

Samuel Palmer

86. SHEEP-SHEARING

H. Reitlinger, Esq.

J. S. Cotman

Mrs. Esmond Morse

87.   THE MARKET-PLACE, NORWICH

is said that at Strathfieldsaye alone there are an immense number of his works, which have never been looked at since the great Duke of Wellington had them rolled up and consigned to the darkness. Drawings by Fuseli of the quality of The Toilet must be rare; but there may be others. It is hardly probable that it stands alone.

Some reference has already been made in this book to the contact between Fuseli and William Blake. It affected only one phase of either artist. It is Fuseli at his worst, and it is certainly not William Blake at his best. The Blake of the Prophetic Books and of the Book of Job is the correction, if it can be said so, of this comparison. But we come now to a disciple of William Blake, of whom it can only be said that he possessed, in all probability, the most poetical temperament of any English painter there has ever been. This is Samuel Palmer. At the age of nineteen, in 1824, he made the acquaintance of Blake, then an old man nearly seventy years of age and within three years of his death. Blake, who was one of the four or five greatest poets in our language, had an extreme personal radiance which affected and inspired, not only Palmer, but another young artist, Edward Calvert, as well. Blake had lately published his woodcut illustrations to Dr. Thornton's *Virgil*. These tiny works, only an inch or two in dimension, and published in wretched form, were the prophecies of a new pastoral or bucolic world of poetry. The Eclogues and Georgics of Virgil were transferred by Blake to an Arcadian peace and simplicity of sacred groves and vales. Soon after their meeting, Samuel Palmer, who was delicate all his life, moved down to the country at Shoreham, near Sevenoaks. Here he lived for four or five years, until after the death of his master, being frequently visited by Calvert, by Richmond, Oliver Finch, and others of the band of enthusiasts who had gathered round the aged William Blake. Calvert, whom we may dismiss here in a couple of sentences, for his works cannot enter into the category of this book, was to produce under the influence of those woodcuts to *Virgil* his own rare and lovely woodcuts and engravings. These include The Cyder Feast, The Lady and the Rooks, The Chamber Idyll, all of them works which are absolutely unique and original and instinct with poetry to an extent that is without parallel, except in the case of his friend and companion Samuel Palmer.

During the years of his stay at Shoreham this young man would seem to have been in an ecstasy of poetical sensitiveness and appreciation. It would be akin to the religious ecstasies of ascetics and is to be found nowhere else except in mysticism and in poetry. He drew and painted continually, read poetry, and went for moonlight walks in the country round. The landscape became transfigured and altered by the ecstasy of his appreciation. A large number of water-colour drawings show him in this poetical or imaginative trance. Their titles, The Bright Cloud, The Rising Moon, Opening the Fold, will give their pastoral quality. The shapes of chestnut and elm take on new significance in his drawings. There are, indeed, bright clouds lying against, as if bellying their white or sunlit sails upon the blossoming fruit boughs. The sheepfolds are like primitive village forms upon the hillsides, while the grazing flocks are seen with a fresh vision as though they were domestic animals, newly tamed in magnanimity and kindness. Hills are rounded like the knolls of English parkland and then, suddenly, through the chestnut leaves, the shelving hilltop is seen with a shepherd leaning on his crook and looking down into the vale below. This is, in itself, a pastoral or poetical conceit. The seasons are simple and Arcadian in their divisions, ruled to the flocks. Houses are thatched with reeds and the image of mankind is in the shepherd and the shepherdess.

More rare still than his drawings are the very few oil paintings that Samuel Palmer accomplished during this transcendental time. It is probable, indeed, that not more than six or eight of these are in existence. They are as closely related in subject as his water-colour drawings, being in the nature of imaginative variations upon the pastoral or bucolic theme. Three or four paintings, together with a number of drawings, are still, or were until lately, in the possession of a lady and her brother who are descended from friends of the artist. One of these pictures, which is described as being in oils upon varnished paper, bears a very close resemblance to the beautiful painting in the collection of Mr. Henry Reitlinger which we are enabled to reproduce (86). It is, in fact, another disposition and arrangement of the same material. But the picture that we are now describing is painted upon a thick oaken board, or even upon part of the wooden door of a barn. It is so heavy that it requires the strength of two men in order to lift it down from the wall where it hangs. This was to be a primitive pastoral subject, and Samuel Palmer was determined to make it so by every means in his power. The oaken board was in exact accord with his serious and laborious intention.

This painting, in spite of its heaviness to lift, is small in size. It is most lyrical in effect. The first impression that it gives is that of an extra-ordinary golden quality of colour. A ripe cornfield, and more especially the ripened oats, have this golden tonality, which is that of the slanted sun. Its subject is sheep-shearing, and the shepherds and shepherdesses are seen through a rustic archway that is formed through an opening in

J. M. W. Turner

88. THE HOE, PLYMOUTH

The Victoria and Albert Museum

the wall of a barn. This picture is painted, as it were, upon a portion of the wooden wall of this pastoral building. The opened doors of the barn give on to the golden landscape, through which this oaten or corn-yellow light advances and illumines the wooden temple. For a sacred importance, a kind of bucolic holiness has been given to this humble building. These are the shepherd kings, or the kings of the golden corn-land. Yet the picture has no conscious archaisms, although its very existence is purely in terms of poetry. But the barn has become the temple, or shrine, of the pastoral ritual. Its details, or symbols, are like trophies of arms. They are formed of rakes and flails, of the sickle and the gleaner's basket. Its plaited straw is in allusion to the harvest. The harvest light fills every corner of the painting. As for the landscape, which is to be seen through the wide open doors of the barn, it is entirely transmuted through the medium of poetry. It would only be at rare moments, as rare as the breath of inspiration, that the declining light, the spectrum of a rainbow, or the silver frost can give these exceptional and transitory appearances. It is this momentary and passing poetry that Samuel Palmer has brought into prominence. The golden glow which for a moment, and for a moment only, comes from the slope of the hillside into the humble wooden barn, it is this which the painter has made into the common tenour, or the ordinary truth of existence.

For three or four years Samuel Palmer was able to sustain himself in this state of spiritual and poetical exaltation. The trance, or mirage, of Edward Calvert was not less remarkable. Only one small painting by him, dating from this period, is known to be in existence; but The Cyder Feast, the best of his engravings, is entirely in the personal canon of Samuel Palmer. The lack of information upon the detail of Palmer's stay at Shoreham is the more deplorable, for the two painters were in constant association together. It would be interesting, for instance, to discover whether the poetry of Keats, so lately published, had come their way. There is nothing, nothing whatever, of the prevailing Byronic tendencies in either Palmer or Calvert. Their work forestalls, and just as surely surpasses, that of the Pre-Raphaelites. Just as surely as Keats anticipates, by forty years, the quintessence or real excellence of that movement, so does Samuel Palmer point to what could have been, and never was, achieved by their painters. These few works by the 'Ancients,' as their friends called the disciples of William Blake, are the only pictures or smaller works that have kept in harmony and intention with the major glories of our poetry. To look from Palmer or from Calvert to Blake or to Keats is no declension nor disparagement. To turn from Turner to Byron, or from Millais to

Tennyson, is a process in which both concerned suffer and are revealed in their weaknesses.

After these few years of poetical afflatus neither Samuel Palmer nor Calvert ever fulfilled themselves again. They lived to old age, dying in 1881 and 1883, respectively. Both men lived quietly and undemonstratively, continuing in their ways, but the inspiration had left them. A glance at the edition of Virgil's *Eclogues* translated and illustrated by Samuel Palmer will prove this. It was published after Palmer's death, but had occupied him, at intervals, for many years of his life. This is a graceful but entirely spiritless work, lacking entirely all those qualities of inspiration which he had possessed during those few wonderful years when he was between the ages of nineteen and twenty-five. There is danger, unfortunately, that this neglected artist may receive the unwelcome attentions of any modern iconoclast who may be looking round for support for his theories. There is much that could be said about him, and it may be spoken by those who are the least appropriate to say it. Samuel Palmer could be made without much trouble into the Gerard Manley Hopkins of English painting. And, if that is done, followers as unworthy of him, and as unbespoken, may impute their faults and their glaring inconsistencies to his memory.

It will be some indication of the latent possibilities in both Fuseli and Samuel Palmer that, for some considerable time, this book must content itself with the stray productions of little-known or unlikely painters. The Market Place at Norwich, by J. S. Cotman, is a specimen by that artist into which more human observation has entered than was his general wont. We may imagine, if it pleases us, that George Borrow is one of that East Anglian assembly gathered round the market stalls and in front of the inns. The Horse Fair at Melton Mowbray (89), by John Ferneley, demands a place immediately after this. This is a beautiful example of equine painting, enlivened by any number of figures of men and women. This, also, thinking again of George Borrow, was no more than a two days' walk from Norwich, and that tireless pedestrian is illustrated once more, as it were, among the onlookers at the Horse Fair. The Old Hampton Ferry (90), by W. Havell, is a nearly unique example of painting in oils on the part of one of the most famous of our water-colour and aquatint school. William Havell drew the plates for a magnificent publication upon the river Thames, and, as well, accompanied Lord Amherst's mission to China, proceeding afterwards to India, where he practised his art with success. Several books upon India and China are illustrated with aquatints from his drawings. He took up oil painting upon his return to England, after 1825, and this picture must date from about that period in his life. There

89.   THE HORSE FAIR, MELTON MOWBRAY

John Ferneley

Private Collection, America

W. Havell

90. THE OLD HAMPTON FERRY

The Redfern Galleries

are more miscellaneous things pertaining to this time. The Schoolmistress (93), by John Opie, is an unusual, if not particularly interesting picture. The Return from the Fair (92), by Thomas Webster, hardly, perhaps, deserves inclusion, but it is entirely characteristic of its time and is by a painter who was responsible for an immense number of pictures of sentiment, some of which achieved huge popularity. Two paintings by Mulready that follow upon this (94, 95) are delightful things of their kind by a man who was a genuine artist. On the other hand, The Travelling Showman (107), by William Kidd, an altogether unknown painter, is not inferior to these. A Girl at a Waterfall (81), by Maclise, is a pleasing subject by one of the most delightful of book illustrators. All those who know his drawings for the poems of Thomas Moore will agree with this. The one Irishman was a most appropriate interpreter for the other. And finally, in order to close this paragraph with something altogether improbable, there is the Demolition of the Dominican Church at Genoa (85), by Sir Thomas Lawrence. This must have been painted during his travels abroad, after Waterloo, the proof of which date is in the costumes worn by the figures. It is more difficult to determine what can have induced him to paint it. Perhaps a wet day or two in an hotel, with nothing to do, may have been the reason.

The Use of Tears (106), by Bonington, is of interest in this context because of its nearness to The First Earring (102), a most beautiful little painting by Sir David Wilkie. Its shockingly damaged condition is only too visible in the photograph. Sir David Wilkie is further shown in two fine paintings, The Village School at Pitlessie (104) and Reading the Will (103). The second of these has almost the stillness and perfection of an early daguerrotype, a curious criterion, perhaps, to apply to a work of art. But Sir David Wilkie, who in a subsequent generation might have been an Orchardson, or even a Marcus Stone, offers a convincing proof of the importance of tradition. Where there is tradition, painters of the second or third rank can, at least, be prevented from an absolute descent into limbo.

Where William Etty is concerned it is impossible not to express a feeling of disappointment. Etty is a painter who, between the years 1820 to 1850, has a position entirely to himself, in which no one approaches him. His subject was the nude. Youth at the Prow and Pleasure at the Helm, a beautiful picture and probably his masterpiece, cannot unfortunately find inclusion here, as it is mythological in subject. Etty was lost in admiration of the Venetian painters. He speaks of 'Venice, the birthplace and cradle of colour, the hope and idol of my professional life.' It is sad that a diligent search has only been able to retrieve the Conversation Piece that is illustrated here (91) as being suitable for our context. This little picture is, it would seem, most beautiful in colour. Etty, though, is a painter who will never fail of admirers.

Punch, or May Day (83), by Benjamin Haydon, must be the memorial of that unfortunate painter. It is only too evident from his *Autobiography* that writing was the true form in which the talent of Haydon expressed itself. His account of the Coronation of George IV is not less than wonderful as a piece of writing. He had the gift of phrase to an extreme degree. He describes the moment when the peers and peeresses rise to their feet and put their coronets upon their heads as a 'silken, feathered thunder.' Discoveries of the *mot juste* were made by him in plenty; but never their equivalent in painting. Punch, or May Day, however, is a picture that deserves attention. It is bold and vigorous in handling and makes it the more to be regretted that Haydon should have wasted his time upon historical painting. This misconception of his own talents brought disaster upon him and culminated in his death by his own hand. It must be considered, however, that other, perhaps, smaller paintings of this nature must be in existence and neglected. If the time ever comes for their rediscovery a new view of Benjamin Haydon may be necessary and something of the fame for which he longed be restored to him.

The search for a genre painting by Turner has resulted in a colour plate of Plymouth Hoe (88). This may not be a great picture but it is an enjoyable scene, and the hand of Turner is evident, almost, as it were, in parody of itself. This was ever the case with Turner when his work was not at his highest level of concentration. Like the Hornpipe from Handel's water music, this not completely serious example of the master hand makes a pleasurable occasion. It is, also, in either case, something of a patriotic demonstration. The early fame of Turner was as a sea painter and, in this, he is celebrating a nautical festival on shore.

Having disposed, in the last paragraph or two, of some of the miscellanea of the school, it is now the easier to turn to projects that will have more rewards to offer. There is all the achievement of mid-Victorian painting to discuss; but, before that comes, and because it is in the nature of a throwback, an atavistic suspension or delaying of time, we have the paintings of George Cruikshank. He has been written of already at another part of this book, though that was in general anticipation of his fame. Here his oil paintings, and those only, are to be considered. They have been among the most delightful of revelations when it came to preparing these pages. Cruikshank would seem to have embarked upon oil painting

91. A CONVERSATION

William Etty   *F. F. Madan, Esq.*

92. THE RETURN FROM THE FAIR

T. Webster *The Victoria and Albert Museum*

93. THE SCHOOLMISTRESS

John Opie *A. T. Loyd, Esq.*

94. THE FIGHT INTERRUPTED

William Mulready   *The Victoria and Albert Museum*

95.   THE CONVALESCENT FROM WATERLOO

William Mulready   *The Victoria and Albert Museum*

96.   GRIMALDI SHAVED BY A GIRL

George Cruickshank

97.   THE DISTURBER DETECTED

George Cruickshank

in about 1855, when he was sixty-three years of age. The height of his achievement had come in the 'thirties and 'forties of the century. It is to be supposed that the failure of his *Comic Almanack*, which had run for so long, and the unsuccess of his *Fairy Library*, though that was among the most imaginative of all his productions, had left him in the determination to make one last effort for popularity. These two disappointments had occurred in 1852 and 1853, which makes our theory more plausible. It must be remembered that George Cruikshank, by the 'fifties of the century, was in that position sometimes encountered by artists in which the extent of their activities has become so great, and their fame so universal, that it is taken for granted, and the support of the public is gradually withdrawn, as from something that is already so established that it is moribund. A parallel instance is in the case of Liszt, who had published so much music that it became a superfluity, until eventually his latest and best pieces attracted no attention whatever. This is exactly the situation of George Cruikshank.

He began, then, first of all, with some small subjects which were in the nature of experiments, in order to try his hand. Within a year or two he was painting the pictures that are here reproduced. Some few of his pictures are outside our scope, such as his Cinderella, a sort of fairy phantasmagoria, which is in the Victoria and Albert Museum. The Runaway Knock (8), however, is Cruikshank at his most suitable and, it is as certain, at his best. This painting is upon a heavy wooden panel. In its minor and unpretentious manner nothing could be more charming than this picture. The fat footman is one of Cruikshank's most lifelike inventions. The children have knocked at the door and run away, and he comes out having just woken up and put on his coat. Needless to say, he looks into the wrong direction. Meanwhile, a horde of eight dogs has escaped into the road and the parlour window is crowded with faces, and with a cockatoo, all looking out in alarm. The house, it may be said, is just such a one as the local authorities would, by now, have condemned for destruction. It is, that is to say, a quite beautiful small Georgian house, most comfortable and pleasant to live in. The hollyhock, the flower-pots on the window-sill, and the creeping vine are in emphasis upon this comfort, which is further graced by a most beautiful overdoor and fanlight window to match.

The Disturber Detected (97), which was bought by the Prince Consort, and is now at Windsor Castle, is not less delightful. The fearful figure of Cruikshank's beadle is here immortalized in paint. Terror is inimitably expressed in the small boy's features. The occupants of the family pew are startled, but not seriously annoyed. The fat little boy of the family, who is too small to see over the top of the pew, and is therefore imprisoned in it, is a charming point of the picture; and so is the old maidservant peering over the back of the pew. This is, in fact, an early Victorian Sunday morning to the life. The tombs and emblazoned heraldry of that village church only lend emphasis to this little moment out of its long life.

The Ghost (98) is what could be most facilely described as a powerful study in black and white. It would appear to date from an early period in Cruikshank's life, and is given here among his oil paintings in order to show the proportions to which he could attain by the most simple means. Immediately after this we come to Grimaldi in a Barber's Shop (96). This is a small picture and was painted by Cruikshank as a present to an American friend of his who was as ardent a temperance worker as himself. We are told that it was delivered to him just before he left London on his journey home. The year in all probability was 1856. This same friend, who was born in London and went early in life to America, has left a description of a day spent with Cruikshank revisiting their old haunts of childhood together. In the course of this, Cruikshank took him to Sadler's Wells Theatre, where, thirty years before, Grimaldi used to play. A morning or two later, when Sunday came round, Cruikshank called for him and they went to see Grimaldi's grave at Pentonville. It seems, in fact, as if Cruikshank must have painted this picture after one of their conversations together. It depicts a scene from Dickens' *Life of Grimaldi*. The same incident had been drawn by Cruikshank twenty years before, in illustration of that book, but this oil painting is quite different. It shows us Grimaldi as a young, dark-haired man, and must give us the veritable action of his hands and feet when singing a song. In fact, this precious document is the best portrait extant of the greatest of clowns. The accessories in the picture are a delight in themselves, from the portrait of the Iron Duke over the fireplace to the exquisitely dandified figure of the friend who is waiting for Grimaldi. This friend is in a paroxysm of laughter, as are the barber and his assistant. No one, in short, will claim that this picture is a major work of art, but it is a most valuable historical document and, certainly in the writer's opinion, must be one of the most enviable of personal possessions.

After a short period spent in painting such pictures as those just described Cruikshank embarked upon what he intended to be the great work of his life. This is his immense Worship of Bacchus (99). It is the culmination of his temperance work and occupied him for some two to

98. THE GHOST

George Cruickshank

George Cruickshank

99. THE WORSHIP OF BACCHUS

The National Gallery

three years of his life. In addition, he completed the outlines of the figures for an immense engraving of the subject. He was, by now, seventy years of age, but the picture, which was exhibited up and down the country in 1862-3, failed as a financial project. This, in reality, marked the end of his active career. He lived for another fifteen years, until 1878, but no commissions for drawings came to him, although he was still prepared to execute them. A few stray illustrations, and a frontispiece or two, are all that he accomplished, though still in the prime of his energies; but taste had outlived him and his survival into the 'sixties and 'seventies was an anachronism. The Worship of Bacchus might have won the popularity of Frith's Derby Day. It cannot be called a picture. It is a mosaic of small illustrations in oil; many of the groups being charming, or dramatic, in themselves. If taken in isolation, one by one, or enlarged, they contain some most realistic scenes of Victorian life, which deserve the attention of the social historian; but, as a work of art, The Worship of Bacchus is a complete failure, and it could not be otherwise. Now it lingers gloomily in the subterranean vaults of the National Gallery. When enquired for this summer, the picture was covered thickly with the dust of generations. Only three persons had asked for it in the last thirty-five years and, in the case of two of those, it was to obtain the measurements of the picture in order to win a bet.

If The Runaway Knock, or Grimaldi in a Barber's Shop, can be claimed almost as discoveries in this book, they can be succeeded immediately by the discussion of Richard Dadd, for he must remain the most interesting personality of these pages. The peculiar circumstances of his life, which shrouded him in total obscurity, have reduced the mention of his name to a mere line or two, or a couple of sentences, in any of the books that deal with English painting. It is time, therefore, that sympathetic hands should lift the curtain, and the tragic drama of his fate must be our excuse for devoting more space to him than can merely accompany the two of his pictures here reproduced. Richard Dadd, then, was born at Chatham in 1817, the son of a prosperous chemist. He gave early signs of talent and was taken by his parents to London for greater opportunities of study. One of his fellow-students was Frith, who has left touching mention of him in his Autobiography. At about twenty-three years of age Dadd went on a voyage to the East with Lord Foley. It seems probable that he got sunstroke while in Egypt, and the first premonitory symptoms of his malady appear in letters written from that country to Frith. He must have come home in precarious condition, because Frith again intimates that he has received appalling news, as a result of which he is in misery about his friend. He returns to London, sees Frith, and talks gaily, appearing to be in the best of health. A few weeks later his father takes him down to the country, this is in May 1847, and they arrive for the night at Cobham, at the White Lion Inn. The inn is full and the waiter says rooms can be found in the village. Mr. Dadd orders a room for two persons, with the words 'It is my son, you know,' and the son says, gruffly, 'You had better get two rooms.' After this they have supper and go out together for a walk. They never return that night.

The next day the body of a man is found, stabbed to the heart, near the edge of a deep pit in Cobham Wood. The first news is brought to the inn, where the waiter guesses the tragedy at once, and goes running for a doctor. Some days later Richard Dadd is apprehended in France, near Fontainebleau, carrying on him, it is said, a list, with drawings, of prominent persons who deserved death. There is also a story that in the train on the way to Paris he had decided to kill his fellow-passenger had it been a stormy sunset, but the sun went down clear and fine and so he spared his life. Dadd was brought to England, and as the result of legal proceedings was put under restraint for the rest of his days. This, it will be remembered, was in 1843, and the wretched man lived till 1887, for nearly half a century more. First of all, and for many years, Bedlam was his home and, after that, Broadmoor. During all this lifetime he saw no one of the outside world and cannot have known what was proceeding in the world of art. Owing, it is said, to the kindness of a daughter of the Governor he was allowed his drawing materials, and he even achieved a few oil paintings upon a considerable scale. But it is chiefly his drawings that are remarkable. So rare, though, are his works that it will be possible to enumerate, in a sentence or two, all the good drawings or paintings by Dadd met with since his name was first heard by the writer, twenty years ago.

Of his oil paintings we reproduce The Fairy-Teller's Master-Stroke (100), which has now been put on loan at the Ashmolean Museum at Oxford. This is a picture which, even in the reproduction, repays long and careful study. It is in that peculiar and minute technique which was the secret of Dadd, and particularly suited, in this instance, to the subject. This crowded scene, or phantasmagoria, all takes place in the world of dew. The long tassels of blades of corn interrupt the entire picture and give scale to its minutiæ of imagination. The fallen hazel-nuts rise waist-high and, even then, this world of raindrop and green leaf has personages so infinitely small that they can hardly be seen at all. It is impossible to determine the subject, because the whole point of this picture is its con-fusion of existences and in its revelation of little miniature worlds hidden

100.   THE FAIRY-TELLER'S MASTER STROKE

Richard Dadd

Siegfried Sassoon, Esq.

Richard Dadd   The Fairfeller's Master-Stroke

101. IN A CURIOSITY SHOP

under the leaves. We can draw attention, but without attempting to explain, to this world of figures and will begin, for this purpose, from the top of the picture. There is a man in a farmer's smock; below him, on the left, a knife-grinder; a straw-hatted woman; a soldier in a cocked hat, with the staring expression that is characteristic of the painter; a man blowing a trumpet and, in fact, an arabesque of trumpets hangs in the air above his head, below the thistle-heads; the king and queen of a fairy story with, on the left, the tiny, almost microscopic figure of an old witch in red cloak and black steeple or Welsh hat, who appears to be cursing them as she leans upon her stick; much below, on the left, two splendid and beautiful women, in full short skirts, pleated and almost like a dancer's skirts; a terrifying, blind old man with an immense head, sitting at their feet, as in a fit of despondent insanity; next to him, a nightmare lover and his batlike inamorata, horribly distorted in feature, like faces in a distorting glass; on their right two more appallingly bloated or distended figures; under the skirts of the two dancers, two more dancers looking silently; below them, on the left, two microscopic dwarfs, or pucks; a bearded man and his wife with Spanish or gypsy curls; on their right, some ordinary, everyday workmen hewing with axes, one of them, his hands on his knees, gazing raptly into nothing with that same staring expression of the eyes; above, on the right, two handsome bearded men in plumed cavalier hats, one of them playing on the mandoline; and, looking from them, to the left once more, above those bloated and distorted figures, there would appear to be the face of God; and then, again, above the nightmare lovers, in top-hat and clothes of the 'forties, of that time when Dadd last saw the living world of men and women, there are some little evil, winged Cupids; and the eyes, then, lose themselves in still more minute worlds, with friezes of little figures hiding away among the leaves. Such is an account of The Fairy-Teller's Master-Stroke. Its meaning it is impossible to know, but this important work by the only good painter who worked through a lifetime of mental disease deserves every thought and attention. It is even painted as though it were an introduction to the world of the subconscious.

This may be said of all Dadd's works, that no two of them are alike. The other drawing (101) by his hand, here reproduced, is scarcely to be recognized as the work of the same hand. It is one of a set done to illustrate the human passions. There are one or two curious points to be noticed about this drawing, more particularly the gilt spurs worn by the man who is examining the picture on the easel. This detail is in the nature of an obstinate irrelevancy, and we may begin to observe here something which is typical and, perhaps, symptomatic of Dadd. It is the odd expression of the eyes. The eyelids are always sharply cut and there is a cruel stare in the pupils. The drawing in question is not, it may be added, at all distinguished among his works. In fact, the series illustrating the passions are, so to speak, the commonplaces of his art. But now, for the first time upon any printed page, there occurs the opportunity to speak of the rest of his achievement.

If we revert for a moment to The Fairy-Teller's Master-Stroke, which has already been described and illustrated, it is to call attention to its companion picture, which disappeared many years ago and is said now to be in a private collection in Leeds. His works are so rare that this mention of a missing picture must be its own excuse. It is a painting in the form of a roundel, and the subject, which is reported to be taken from *A Midsummer Night's Dream*, relates it to the Fantasy to which it was pendent. Almost the only other known oil painting by Dadd must be the large oriental scene in the author's possession. This is crowded with hundreds of figures in every variety of Bedouin dress, who are gathered in an encampment of tents in the desert. Some figures in crusading armour are in their midst; but the picture, in default of some title, or more precise indication, is quite beyond explanation. At the same time these innumerable figures, posed in groups which are done in greatest detail but have no relationship to each other, have the breath of insanity upon them. This picture, which is signed and dated Bethlehem Hospital 1849, 1850, may be the largest and most important oil painting by Dadd that is in existence. There only remains his portrait of his keeper, a small painting which was shown this summer at the Victorian Exhibition at the Leicester Galleries. It is certainly a most curious production. A young man, much too mild in appearance to be a keeper, is sitting on a rustic garden seat, made of logs of wood. A red fez reposes by his side. At his back there is some giant plant, perhaps a sunflower, with immense leaves upon which the microscopic dewdrops can be seen. In the distance there is a garden roller and a summer-house. This picture of suburban London in the 'fifties is painted in the technique of a Flemish primitive, but seen with Surrealist insistence upon the irrelevant.

We come now to his drawings. The best of these form a division to themselves in English painting. They are exquisite in perfection and so minute in execution that they must have been done in a fever of nervous concentration. A drawing, called Port Straggling, which was left by Mr. Robert Ross to the British Museum, must be his masterpiece. It portrays in incredible detail an immense rock, suggested perhaps by the Rock of

102. THE FIRST EARRING

Sir David Wilkie

The Tate Gallery

Sir David Wilkie

103.   READING THE WILL

Sir David Wilkie

104. THE VILLAGE SCHOOL AT PITLESSIE

Major Philip Fleming

105.   NEWSMONGERS

Sir David Wilkie   *The Tate Gallery*

Gibraltar which Dadd must have seen when on his travels, beneath which lies a harbour town crowded with shipping and with its streets alive with figures. All this is done in his stippled technique with the point of the brush. At the back of the drawing is a long and insanely meaningless inscription in his hand. The drawing is dated in the 'sixties. Another lovely drawing is the Italian Wandering Musicians, which belongs to Mr. Richard Wyndham. It is dated as late as 1878, probably the last good drawing by his hand. A shepherd, a young girl with a mandoline and a small boy with a pipe, are in a classical landscape strewn with fragments of sculpture. This is a realistic vision of some scene he had seen in the East, in Ionic Greece, just as the large painting of the Oriental scene, just noticed, is the evocation of his travels in Egypt when his mind began to be affected, as can be proved in the extracts from his letters in Frith's *Autobiography*. There must also be mentioned a drawing of a Yacht Race, in the Tate Gallery, a naturalistic phantasmagoria which recalls the glass ships under glass domes, dear to the early Victorians; one or two Egyptian drawings of dervishes or Arab scribes; a combat of men in armour, a Biblical subject, incredible in invention of detail, belonging to Mr. Osbert Sitwell; an Oriental scene at the Ashmolean Museum, Oxford, signed Monsieur R. Dadd and dated in the 'fifties, like Liotard in its figures, enlivened with an exquisite drawing of a black and white cat, but with an architectural background more reminiscent of the Alhambra of Leicester Square than the authentic Alhambra of Granada; and, finally, a drawing of a group of children, which, in its curious way, is not less remarkable than any of those described. This must represent nearly the sum total of his existing works, for, at one time, any drawings which came into the market were bought up and destroyed by the too zealous conscience of those who remembered him. There is, nevertheless, at a certain place in the country, a box reputed to contain not less than ten or twelve of his works, and this exciting box should certainly be opened by its owner before the drawings perish from neglect.

Richard Dadd, it must be concisely said, was one of the two or three most interesting of our painters during the nineteenth century. His cruel fate, which cut him off from his fellow-men when only twenty-six years of age, and left him in isolation for another forty years and more, make of him an isolated figure to whom there is no parallel in painting. Any personal information about him is entirely lacking. So far as the writer knows there are only two contemporary mentions of him, one in the *Art Journal*, and one in a Life of Rossetti and his circle, where W. M. Rossetti is reported as having visited him in Bedlam and seen him at work on one of his drawings.

It is not possible, therefore, to know what news came to him of his own contemporaries and what notion, if any, he may have had of the progress of painting. The strong Pre-Raphaelite tendencies that he developed would seem to have been evolved independently and in ignorance of the brotherhood, or of the writings of Ruskin. His sister married Philips, the painter of Spanish scenes, but we do not know to what extent he was kept supplied, during those forty-five years, with books or pictures. All we know, from his friend and fellow-student, Frith, is that Dadd was the most gentle and lovable of beings and that the appalling personal tragedy in which he was involved threw all who knew him into misery and consternation. The outside world he cannot have seen during this long incarceration; neither is there any evidence as to his real condition. He seems to have seized upon every pretext and to have concentrated all his energies upon his pictures or drawings as his only means of escape from the dreadful realities by which he was surrounded. The Fairy-Teller's Master-Stroke, in the few square inches of which it is composed, does really create a whole world or universe, but of a strange and, it will be readily admitted, of a haunted kind. We wonder, when looking at this picture, whether the work of his contemporary Grandville, the French illustrator, was known to him. There is a touch of Grandville in its invention, while Grandville also, it must be related, passed the end of his days in a similar isolation from the world. There may be those still living who could enlighten us upon at least the last years of this unhappy existence, and it is much to be wished that they would come forward and speak, for the time has come when Dadd can be written of apart from the associations which might cling to his name. It is nearly a hundred years ago now since that dreadful day in 1843, and the partner in that terrible deed must be lifted out of the cloud that engulfed him. Of the signs of his disease it is difficult to see any traces, other than in that curious expression of the eyes which we have noticed, and in the meaningless proximity of his figures. He would appear to have had three periods of productivity: one soon after his arrival in Bedlam towards 1850; another late in the 'sixties; and a third and last phase after he was removed to Broadmoor, of which the Italian Wandering Musicians may be typical. But this can only be studied when more information is available and a wider search has been made for his pictures and drawings.

The Pre-Raphaelites are now imminent, but before we come to them, an older man who shared in many of their principles must be considered. This is J. F. Lewis, or 'Spanish' Lewis, as he was more generally known. He was born in London in 1803, one of a numerous family of painters of German origin who had Anglicized their name from Ludwig. He showed

106.   THE USE OF TEARS

R. P. Bonington

Museum of Fine Arts, Boston

107. THE TRAVELLING SHOWMAN

William Kidd   *The Parker Galleries*

108. CADOGAN PIER, CHELSEA

G. W. Brownlow   *The Leicester Galleries*

precocious talents as a child, and by the age of twenty was already a gifted painter of animals. He was then employed for some two years by George IV at Windsor, where he painted many animal and sporting pictures, of which the best is probably that of the Royal Buckhounds in Windsor Great Park, which picture has lately been exhibited in the Tate Gallery. This painting is one of the finest examples of a sporting subject, in that branch of painting in which Alken and J. F. Herring excelled. But J. F. Lewis was not contented and, resigning this employment, proceeded to Scotland, where he worked upon the landscape of the Highlands. After this came his Spanish phase, when he lived for some years in Seville and Granada, and is, in fact, the painter of the First Carlist War, the Proclamation of Don Carlos being his chief picture of this period. Two books of lithographs from his Spanish drawings were published.

In 1838, 1839, Lewis was in Constantinople and in Asia Minor. Many water-colours date from this time, and he lithographed a book of sketches from the drawings of an amateur of which the subject was Constantinople. By slow stages he then proceeded to Egypt, where he was to remain for not less than ten years, 1841-51. During most of this time he sent nothing home and was, in fact, lost sight of by his contemporaries. Thackeray has left a description of him living in native style in Cairo. But in 1850 he sent back for exhibition at the Old Water-colour Society, The Hhareem, the first of his works in which his new principles were apparent. It was said at the time, and this is probably still true, that The Hhareem is the most extraordinary work ever executed in water-colours. As a study of light drifting in minute particles, or sun motes, through a screen of lattices, this drawing exceeds in minute accuracy anything that has ever been attempted. This drawing was followed in 1852 by An Arab Scribe; and then, in rapid succession, by The Well in the Desert, The Greeting in the Desert, and A Frank Encampment in the Desert. Of this latter drawing, Ruskin, who had now rallied with enthusiasm to his support, wrote: 'In the sky, even, the whole field is wrought gradually out with touches no larger than the filaments of a feather—in fact, it is an embroidered sky.' The School at Cairo and The Prayer of Faith were two more drawings of this nature. Whole months were spent by Lewis upon a single drawing of a few square inches. The problem of remuneration was made impossible by this over-minuteness, and in the end even Ruskin had to exhort him not to waste himself altogether upon this Lilliputian scale.

By this time Lewis had himself decided upon the same policy and, returning to England, he took up oil painting in 1858, and persevered

75

with that until his death in 1876. It is from this time, therefore, that his large paintings date; though they are carried out in something of the same elaboration which distinguished his water-colours. They consist, almost exclusively, of Egyptian scenes, but are rendered according to the Pre-Raphaelite prescription. It is superfluous to say about them, as did Ruskin of his earlier water-colours, that nothing finer had been done since Paul Veronese. And yet they are exceptional works done by a painter of peculiar tact and sensibility, and possessed of a degree of patience which is nearly incredible. Lewis, who began as an Alken, or J. F. Herring, and then drew the most romantic of Spanish drawings excelling Dévéria, or any French romantic painter, became, first of all, the great Oriental water-colour painter of the century. There are Oriental drawings by J. F. Lewis, touched in lightly with washes of blue or light red, that are as delicate as any pastel by Liotard, and, in addition, Lewis was an adept at drawing architecture. Mosques and minarets are seen through his perforated lattices; there is the play of fountains and the shimmer of fine silks. Perhaps the time has not yet come for an exhibition of this painter's works; but it is one of the last of minor sensations in reserve for our jaded palates. The late Colonel Lawrence, it may be added, was a great admirer of J. F. Lewis and had often discussed the possibility of organizing such an exhibition. Lewis was that rare and unusual phenomenon, a painter of Oriental scenes who was also an artist. Where Chinnery failed J. F. Lewis succeeded. Not that his paintings are in any sense wilfully Oriental in their technique. Lewis is not to be compared in this to that greatest of all pasticheurs, the Jesuit Castiglione, who lived for so long in Pekin at the Court of Kien Lung, and became so entirely assimilated that his paintings are only distinguished by their signature from the works of the Chinese painters of that last decadence. Castiglione was an exquisite painter of the Italian rococo, a Longhi, or a Guardi, absorbed into another tradition; J. F. Lewis was a painter with the point of view of a naturalist, a trait which was not uncommon among the painters of the Victorian era. But, in addition to this, he had great and solid powers of composition, while retaining all the slighter graces which are so charmingly displayed in his water-colours of Spain, or of Asia Minor, before his work took on its serious and too laborious aspects.

With J. F. Lewis disposed of, the Pre-Raphaelite Brotherhood must now claim our attention. It would be tedious to tell all over again of the foundation of their society. If Dante Gabriel Rossetti was the inspiring force behind it, the most conscientious practitioner of its principles, there can be no doubt, was Holman Hunt, who all through his long life adhered

109. LILIUM AURATUM

J. F. Lewis

J. F. Lewis

110. INDOOR GOSSIP

C. W. Dyson Perrins, Esq.

to its ideals and never forsook them, as did Millais, in order to achieve a more facile success. The great contribution of Holman Hunt to the movement was his painting of The Hireling Shepherd (10). This large and important picture dates from 1854. However much it may be disliked by many persons this painting remains a remarkable performance, more especially when it is considered that Holman Hunt was a young man of twenty-six at the time. He had proceeded to its composition with the utmost and most painstaking care. It is this alone which will make the picture distasteful to an age of irrelevance and speed. The landscape was painted in Surrey, though the two versions he made of it, thus doubling his laborious task, differ considerably in detail. Almost every object in this picture is made to tell a story. For instance, the butterfly on the girl's lap signifies her light and fickle character; the green apple she has half eaten shows the temptation to which she is succumbing, while even the fact that it is green and unripe holds a message of immaturity and over-eagerness; the sheep, some of whom have strayed, untended by her, into a cornfield which they are spoiling and trampling down, they also have their significance to the story; while we may feel sure that the sheep-dog in one version is, in a sense, the hero of the piece with its alert faithfulness to duty.

As a morality picture The Hireling Shepherd is, of course, jejune and absurd. Holman Hunt was serious-minded to the point of being ridiculous. No humour whatever seems to have entered into his character. But The Hireling Shepherd, all the same, is remarkable by the very excess of its own faults. And they are errors of narrative taste, or of sentiment. The painting, throughout, is admirable and accomplished in a sense in which this is true of but few English paintings. The figures of the shepherd and shepherdess are real and not forced. It is even to be felt how strongly the painter must have disapproved of his model's character, for her way-wardness is implicit in her dreamy, sensuous expression. The bleached, white cornfield and the high and ancient elms have an extraordinary realism to the Surrey landscape. In this sense the picture is comparable to a splendid Constable; but this is not a landscape only, and if we rehearse in our minds the significant paintings of the nineteenth century, it is hard to omit The Hireling Shepherd.

Holman Hunt was never again to approach this unique achievement. His excessive realism was to lead him to ridiculous ends. In painting The Light of the World, he condemned himself to work out of doors, all night, standing in an improvised shelter of sticks and leaves, with his feet in straw to keep them warm during the coldest months of an excessively severe winter. He would start to work at midnight and finish about 5 a.m. All this hardship was undertaken in order to secure an accurate picture of candle or lantern light burning out of the darkness. His companion during this long vigil was a police constable, who often came and talked to him, passing criticism also upon the painting as it proceeded. This is, it may be, not the ideal atmosphere in which a work of art should be created, and perhaps the standards of Holman Hunt became lowered during this process. It could even be suggested, where so fervent a churchman as Holman Hunt was concerned, that the police constable may have been no other than the Dark One, and that the purpose of these midnight conversations was in order to spoil the picture. Instances of the discomfort endured by the painter could be multiplied indefinitely in the case of Holman Hunt. The Scapegoat nearly cost him his life. Perhaps the depths of bathos were reached over this picture. Holman Hunt, for accuracy's sake, had to buy the actual goat which was his model, and it proved to be an animal which gave him infinite trouble. And when, in the end, the forays of the Bedouins made it unsafe for him to camp any longer in the deserts of the Dead Sea, Holman Hunt had to bring back to his studio in Jerusalem not only this restless animal, but also a quantity of the sand in which he had tethered it, in order to be certain that his picture was accurate down to the last detail.

The nerves of Holman Hunt became seriously affected by this incessant strain after the elusive truth. Signs of this tension are to be seen in his paintings. The Flight of the Innocents worried and plagued him into a breakdown. It is painted as though in the light of Bengal flares, and is altogether a horrid and repulsive performance. His pictures did at least, though, bring him immense rewards. Perhaps there has never been an English painter who sold his canvases for such large sums. Out of all this incessant labour there is, unfortunately, but little that can be rescued from oblivion. His painting, The Eve of St. Swithin's, in the Ashmolean Museum, is an atmospheric study of a wet summer day with the rain pattering upon the metal roof of a dovecote. But it is, in fact, the doves and pigeons that make the subject of this picture. At the end of his life Holman Hunt paid a last visit to Jerusalem and painted his immense picture of Easter Day in the Church of the Holy Sepulchre. This painting, which was never sold and remains in the possession of his heirs, is almost the most elaborate of his compositions, but again it fails as a work of art. We reproduce, however, May Morning on Magdalen Tower (9), of which he painted more than one version, which is interesting because, although done by him as late as the 'nineties, it is still in complete accordance with

III. THE LAST OF ENGLAND

Ford Madox Brown

The City of Birmingham Art Gallery

William Dyce   112.   PEGWELL BAY

James Reid

113   HAMPSTEAD HEATH IN 1859

E. R. Kisch, Esq.

114. THE BLACK BRUNSWICKER

Sir John E. Millais

The Lady Lever Art Gallery, Port Sunlight

the first Pre-Raphaelite pictures of forty years before. It is executed in his hard, metallic manner. The flowers, for example, that are strewn round the choristers' feet are like paper blossoms. They bear no relation to real flowers. It is to be felt that this subject was of peculiar fascination to Holman Hunt because it entailed rising at four o'clock in the morning and climbing a long stone stair to the top of a steep tower. Moreover, the service only takes place there once a year, so that, if really conscientious to his principles, the painting of May Morning on Magdalen Tower would have taken a hundred years or more to complete.

The study of all Pre-Raphaelite paintings is, in a way, of morbid and melancholy import. This is particularly the case with The Blind Girl (1) of Millais. The date of this picture is 1856, so that it is almost the last good painting done by Millais. By 1858, at latest, by which time he was no more than thirty years of age, Millais had settled down to the ordinary tenour of his ways. This collapse, or denial, is unforgivable and unpardonable when we look at The Blind Girl. It is a landscape of astonishing beauty and meaning. The symbolism of this picture is, for once, dramatic and worth while. The blind girl, who is tired out with walking, has sat down to rest by the side of the path, at the edge of a golden cornfield. Her very boots are eloquent of her fatigue and of the blundering way in which she is condemned to pass her life. The little companion, who is leading her, hides playfully beneath her cloak and tries to tell her of the magnificent rainbow that has sprung up in the sky behind them. Or, perhaps, she is not even speaking and enjoys the sight for herself. This is a painting of rare poetical quality. It was, also, in its time, an astonishing innovation. There may be no contemporary English painter who has, in our lifetime, produced a picture which has so many of the qualifications of a masterpiece. It is, in the first place, a bold and daring composition with the landscape rising up behind the two figures into the sky, and the rainbow, that fatal temptation to the painter, springing from its fountain foot into the summer air. It is sad and almost unbearable to turn from this to The Black Brunswicker, painted by Millais at almost exactly the same time, for The Black Brunswicker is symptomatic of the depths to which Millais was to fall. He had powers such as have been given to no other English painter, and it is this which makes his very name the subject for melancholy regret.

After Holman Hunt and Millais there must come Ford Madox Brown. He was older, by a few years, than the actual Pre-Raphaelites, and was never actually a member of the Brotherhood, though he remained faithful to its ideals and is to be counted as Pre-Raphaelite in his pictures. Ford Madox Brown was a painter in whom political creeds had taken the place occupied by religion in the case of, for instance, Holman Hunt. Painting, in his view, was to be the servant of political and social doctrines. His famous picture, The Last of England (111), may be taken even as a sermon, or at least as a social parable. The emigrant and his wife, both of whom represent the middle classes at their best, are driven by their poverty into a foreign land. In the background, everyone else on board is either seasick or maudlin. The mix-up of figures in this background, owing to a too con- scientious minuteness over the trivialities of detail, is most characteristic of Madox Brown. But the two main figures, of the emigrant and his wife, could not be better painted, given the limitations of the Pre-Raphaelite manner. The woman's tweed coat is miraculously done, every stitch being shown; while we know, from the evidence of the painter himself, that not less than four weeks were spent by him over her silk scarf, one end of which blows out in the wind. It is almost painful to think that a replica of this picture was also done. That curious little picture Pretty Baa Lambs (12) represents Madox Brown in a different and more lyrical mood. The blue sky and the green spring meadow are beautifully conceived, and the painting, small as it is, has been allowed to proceed at its own pace without insistence upon every blade of grass or every curl of wool upon the lambs' backs. With Work (11) it is a different matter. This was to be the masterwork of Madox Brown, and it occupied many years of his life to complete. It is a scene in Hampstead, of which the site is, or was until a year or two ago, still to be recognized. The picture is meant to exalt the dignity of toil, and no less a figure than that of Thomas Carlyle looks out of the canvas towards the spectator. Madox Brown has left a voluminous account of his motives in composing this crowded composition. But every inch of the canvas has been regarded by the painter with the same focus of the eyes; added to which the ornament of detail has been heaped and piled up until the whole effect is blinding to the eyes. There is no interval of rest at any point in the canvas. Every small object claims an equal share of the attention. But Work, none the less, is a monumental achievement. And the impression that it made during its day must have been one of startling modernity. Nothing of this kind had ever been done before. Its admirers must have seen whole new worlds of possibility thrown open to their thoughts. The grand style could be enlarged into every branch of human activity. There is, indeed, something of the complacency of his contemporary, Macaulay, in this picture. There is the feeling that everything was tending for the best, and that the British working man was as much to be envied as any Norman baron. Unfortunately, these tendencies to a sort of rhapsodic optimism, which were coupled with a

115. THE LAST DAY IN THE OLD HOME

R. B. Martineau

The Tate Gallery

116. THE SLEEPING MODEL

W. P. Frith

Royal Academy Diploma Gallery

117. RAMSGATE SANDS

W. P. Frith

Reproduced by Gracious Permission of H.M. the King

corresponding lack of interest on the part of the public, combined to make a disappointed man of Madox Brown. His later works, the principal of which were civic decorations for Manchester, added nothing to his fame. It is on Work and on The Last of England that his reputation must rest. In these two works, at least, it is secure.

How, though, it may be asked, is Work a great, or almost a great, picture if the same remark does not apply to Frith's Derby Day (119)? It can only be answered by the remark that Derby Day is a panorama upon an immense scale, but not a work of art. To the other two major achievements of Frith, The Railway Station (118) and Ramsgate Sands (117), exactly the same stricture may be applied. They are fascinating as studies of contemporary life, and Ramsgate Sands is, perhaps, a little more than that. But this may be because of adventitious aids, the stucco lodging-houses in the background, or the mere fascination in any picture of the English seaside. But we shall see, very shortly, that another rendering of that subject, which cannot have taken its painter more than a few hours to execute, is a real and genuine work of art, to which the Ramsgate Sands of Frith cannot be compared.

And in the meantime, before we come to that, here is Pegwell Bay (112) by the Scottish painter, William Dyce. This is a picture which may be a favourite with many people, because of its quiet and limpid atmosphere. Dyce was an older man, and this would seem to be an exceptional painting by him. It belongs definitely to the Pre-Raphaelite school, and perhaps diligent search would reveal some other picture by him painted in this manner. In the sky, though it is not visible in the reproduction, there is the great comet of 1858; but the picture has its appeal because of the crinoline dresses, the chalk cliffs, and the black rocks smelling of seaweed.

And now there is the inimitable Augustus Egg, a painter who is not lightly to be despised. The two pictures from Past and Present (123, 124) represent him at the best of his morality Conversation Pieces. The first of the two paintings is not to be surpassed as a mid-Victorian interior, carpets, chairs, tablecloth, all are perfection, and so is the stove-pipe hat reposing on the table. Not much is known of Augustus Egg, except that he was a friend of Charles Dickens and an excellent amateur actor. He painted, chiefly, historical pictures, and these, compared with Past and Present, were a waste of his time. The Last Day in the Old Home (115) by R. B. Martineau is in interesting contrast to Augustus Egg, because here again, as in the case of Frith and Madox Brown, Martineau is not an artist, while Augustus Egg, within his small limitations, is not to be neglected. Another contrast of the same nature is to be seen in Dividend

Day at the Bank of England (23), by an unknown man, G. E. Hicks, compared with The Lowther Arcade (24) by an artist who is not even to be identified. This picture of a toy market is an enchanting thing. The cascade of drums and wooden horses hanging from the ceiling on the right-hand side of the painting is most beautifully done. This, perhaps, tenth-rate work of art could hardly be surpassed, so excellently is it handled, and so much excitement and imagination is imparted to its details. Hampstead Heath (113), by the completely forgotten James Reid, who must have come from Scotland, is another painting which deserves the name. The foreground is most admirably executed, with its ferns and grass and stones. The group of figures is good, too, and so, most certainly, is the far landscape of London with the dome of St. Paul's showing in the distance. A group of elder bushes on the left-hand side gives, not only the year 1859, but even, it may be said, the actual month.

There are, in fact, a whole body of small Victorian paintings which charm by their quaintness and are, then, revealed as being of more than honest workmanship. Instances of the sort could be multiplied indefinitely, though an easy beginning can be made with the water-colour portrait groups which are so numerous, and have nearly always some delightful details of costume or furniture. A more solid example, which must be known to every visitor to the Tate Gallery, is the lady with the wax flowers. She is standing by a table on which the glass dome reposes and her hat, her costume, even the wall-paper, are eloquent of the 'fifties. Another discovery, searching almost at random, is the Cadogan Pier, Chelsea (108), by G. W. Brownlow. This picture has an immediate appeal and requires no elucidation. It is typical of the class of paintings to which we refer. The interior of a bus by W. M. Egley (22), which has been on loan to the Tate Gallery, and is therefore familiar, is still more fascinating. This picture is dated 1859 and is a perfect human document, more interesting and more worth serious study than many a painting with a greater pedigree. It is also a most ingenious piece of work, for every figure must have been separately studied and the whole then fitted together and given its cohesion. W. M. Egley is so little known that it cannot be said whether this is a unique thing, or is representative of his work. In the case of a painter who is so forgotten there may always be the chance that his relatives or descendants may be in possession of more works by his hand. The whole field of these minor Victorian works could be made to yield much more material than its stray investigations have so far brought to light. This Interior of a Bus gives us the real aspect of the age, as no film and no work of fiction can ever restore it to us. The same thing may be said of two drawings (20, 21),

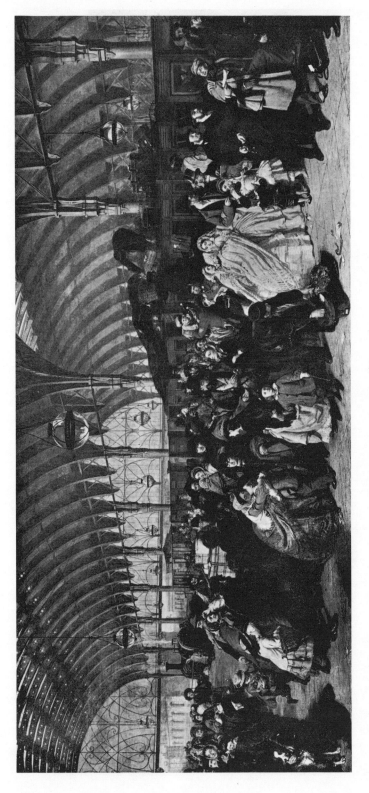

W. P. Frith   118. THE RAILWAY STATION   *Royal Holloway College*

W. P. Frith

119. THE DERBY DAY

The National Gallery

representative of many more, by Eugène Lami. More especially the Scene in Belgrave Square can be studied for indications of the life of the time. The railings and the torch-snuffer alone are indicative of London; the heavy box-seat of the coachman is not less typical; while there are the group of poor women looking on at this departure; the children riding ponies escorted by a bonneted governess and a top-hatted footman; and the Savoyard, or more probably Neapolitan, hurdy-gurdy man, for he wears the peaked hat of the Calabrian, and his hurdy-gurdy, it is quite likely, may be playing *Fra Diavolo* or *Masaniello*. It is to be wished that Lami had left more drawings of life in Eaton, or Belgrave Square. As a Frenchman he had a more objective view of London life.

As climax, or culmination to the 'fifties, there are many works by more serious painters than either Lami or the entirely forgotten men of our last paragraph. A painter like Arthur Hughes provides some of the most complete documentary evidence of his age. In addition to this he was a most charming painter. He would seem to have been of a hard-working but modest and retiring disposition. During the 'fifties he became involved in the secondary wave of Pre-Raphaelites, and their conscientious craftsmanship is reflected in his pictures. Arthur Hughes was also the last survivor of these painters, for he died as lately as 1915. He was one of the best of the book illustrators of the 'sixties, and his work in this medium has a tenderness of sentiment and of imagination that puts him in a class apart from the noisier Frederick Sandys or others of his kind. Here, however, it is his oil paintings that must interest us. April Love (122) is a beautiful little picture which must not be mocked at until, in our generation, we have become as competent ourselves. The blue dress in this painting is lovely in colour. Home from the Sea, at the Ashmolean Museum, is another excellent example of this painter. A young sailor is lying in the grass near the newly covered grave of his mother, we may suppose, who has died while he has been at sea. This, again, is a beautiful little painting. Amy, or The Long Engagement (121) is, it is probable, the most typical work of art of the whole mid-Victorian age. The curate and his betrothed are standing near the tree-stem upon which their joint hands have carved her name. Years have gone by, and still they cannot afford to be married. All round them nature is fulfilling herself. The trees are in leaf; the little red squirrels are playing happily on their branch; even the faithful dog, a symbol so dear to the Victorians, has not, we may understand it, remained celibate; the green moss creeps in a tide up the tree-stem; soon it will engulf that carved inscription. But the curate and his betrothed remain doomed to solitude. It is painted with a weight of sentiment which overbalances into the comical. More especially the time-lag in the curate's dress, for he was a curate, we must remember, of eighty years ago, has given him the dress and appearance of a Mormon preacher, allowing a different interpretation to be put upon the whole picture. And yet, even so, it is genuine sentiment and it is not necessary to be reminded how wretchedly underpaid the minor clergy have always been. This painting is among the most realistically rendered of all the Pre-Raphaelites, vying, in this respect, with Thoughts in a Convent Garden, at the Ashmolean Museum. Its painter was the brother of Wilkie Collins, an artist who died young and could be described as a spasmodic Pre-Raphaelite. The flowers in that picture are even more minutely painted than in The Long Engagement; while the lily pool reveals, among its leaves and stems, a number of tadpoles that increase and diminish with every inspection, so microscopic is their existence. It is to this order of painting that Amy, or The Long Engagement must belong. Nothing more representative of mid-Victorian England could be found; but Arthur Hughes is not to be judged, fairly, upon this picture alone. April Love, or Home from Sea, are specimens of his true achievement.

John Brett belongs to an entirely different order of Pre-Raphaelite. If Madox Brown was Pre-Raphaelite through political feeling, and Arthur Hughes a Pre-Raphaelite by sentiment, this term is only to be applied to John Brett with another import. In any case, it was only true of him for a very few years when he came under the direct, personal influence of Ruskin. The period 1854-60 covers all the Pre-Raphaelite in Brett. Afterwards, he became a good sea painter and was contented with that. His Pre-Raphaelite contribution consists of two pictures; though there must be minor works as well. The Stonebreaker (13), of these two, is the more suitable to our context, and the reproduction in colour makes it superfluous to describe this picture. It was painted in Surrey, Box Hill being in the background. Ruskin says of this picture in his Academy Notes: 'In some points of precision it goes beyond anything that the Pre-Raphaelites have done yet. I know no such thistle-down, no such chalk hills and elm-trees, no such natural pieces of far-away cloud, in any of their work. The composition is palpably crude and wrong in many ways, especially in the awkward white cloud at the top; and the tone of the whole a little too much as if some of the chalk of the flints had been mixed with all the colours. For all that, it is a marvellous picture, and may be examined inch by inch with delight; though nearly the last stone I should ever have thought of anyone's sitting down to paint would have been a chalk flint. If he can make so much of that, what will Mr. Brett not make of mica, slate, and

W. H. Deverell   120.   LADY FEEDING A BIRD   *The Tate Gallery*

121. THE LONG ENGAGEMENT

Arthur Hughes   *The City of Birmingham Art Gallery*

122. APRIL LOVE

Arthur Hughes

The Tate Gallery

Augustus Egg   *The Tate Gallery*

124. PAST AND PRESENT—3

Augustus Egg   *The Tate Gallery*

gneiss! If he can paint so lovely a distance from the Surrey Downs and railway-traversed dales, what would he not make of the chestnut groves of the Val d'Aosta! I heartily wish him good-speed and long exile!'

John Brett was a geological, or even a mineralogical painter. Ruskin, with his mania for geological specimens and his searching in them for the hand of God, must have imagined he had found in Brett the painter for whom he had long been searching. From this point of view The Stone-breaker is an astounding performance. Still more remarkable is the Val d'Aosta, of which we have read the start, as it were, in Ruskin's sententious valedictory phrase. This picture was afterwards bought by Ruskin. In 1858-59 he went to Aosta to help the painter with his advice, though his counsel, typically enough, took the form of encouraging him to greater and greater difficulties of execution. In realism of landscape there is nothing to approach this painting. It is done with the patience of a Flaubert, but without the reward of the sudden and brilliant phrase. The Val d'Aosta seems to have broken Brett's resolution, for it is his last attempt in this direction, much to the chagrin of Ruskin, who wanted him to paint a realistic view of some old Alpine village in a Swiss valley, or in the Tyrol. This ambition of Ruskin was never realized; and realistic painting is the poorer by what might well have been one of the most curious and con-scientious pictures in its annals. It was a subject well suited to Brett's capabilities, for this is an instance in which the doctrines of Ruskin might have borne fruit. Some of the most magnificent passages in Ruskin's writings are those in which he descants upon rock formations, and here was a painter who, had he concentrated upon the genuine directions of his talents, had the ability to achieve things which have never before been attempted. He had the power over minute phenomena of nature, and alike in great rock stratas, in glaciers, or in the dolomitic ravines, which is to be found paralleled in the note-books of Gerard Manley Hopkins, who, also, set about his imposed task with the deliberation of the geological surveyor. A Pre-Raphaelite painter of this precise sort is exactly what is lacking to that movement. It diverted, instead, into the mazes of pretty sentiment, or the insipidities of its third phase, of which Burne-Jones is the representative. But its tendencies, applied scientifically, might have pro-duced some masterpieces of naturalistic observation. Probably this photo-graphic representation is only worth attempting when its very aim is to surpass the camera. The Val d'Aosta is a picture with a two-year exposure, so to speak, and this detailed absorption of nature has been carried to lengths to which the camera cannot follow. Perhaps, therefore, the advice of Ruskin, as we have said, could have been taken profitably in this instance.

John Brett had the beginnings, in a sense, of a Brueghel breadth and attention to detail, in rare combination, and his scientific method might have produced lasting results.

But it is time to part from the Pre-Raphaelites. Scientific realism, of which only The Stonebreaker and the Val d'Aosta are specimens, could have carried the movement into directions where the necessary qualities of patience and of fidelity to fact would have been of more moment than an attentive ear to literature. And yet their painters, even in the first wave of enthusiasm, could achieve such a beautiful little picture as the Lady Feeding a Bird (120). This was painted by Walter Deverell, who died young, and whose other claim to distinction is his discovery of Miss Siddall, who was working in a milliner's shop in Cranbourne Alley, off Leicester Square. It was through Deverell that she met Dante Gabriel Rossetti. This little picture, which is almost all that is left of Deverell, is lovely in colour and most pleasing in subject. It has not that painful care which makes one, in looking at The Stonebreaker, or at the Val d'Aosta, almost pity the person who had to be for so long isolated with his landscape or his heap of flint stones. But, to be able to drag from out of that a picture which has some definite quality is the sign of a higher talent than the easy graces and the sensual prettiness which are the contribution of Walter Deverell. For The Stonebreaker, together with The Blind Girl of Millais, The Hireling Shepherd of Holman Hunt, and Work by Madox Brown, are the four principal pictures of the whole movement, and this judgement differentiates these paintings altogether from the ordinary accepted canons of Pre-Raphaelitism. According to those, it would be Rossetti and Burne-Jones who were the practitioners of the art; but it may have been by now sufficiently proved that scientific realism was its true bent. In this, these paintings connect themselves with those many small and unimportant pictures which are part, unconsciously it is probable, of the whole movement. The Interior of a Bus by W. M. Egley, and the Lowther Arcade by its unidentified painter, belong equally, and as much, to this body or corpus of mid-Victorian painting. To it can be attached, also, the water-colours and oils of J. F. Lewis and the excessively rare works of Richard Dadd. Pegwell Bay, by William Dyce, comes as well into this category. If we include Dyce, it will be necessary also to speak of Frith, a painter inferior to him, as a member of the same group. And, attached to it, as we have said, are all those small and unimportant paintings, some of them by painters whose very names are unknown, and others, of whom the name only remains, and that only because the picture may be signed. Of such is this mid-Victorian school composed, and the sum total of its pro-

Frederick Walker

125. SPRING

The Victoria and Albert Museum

126. SCARBOROUGH SANDS

John Leech   *Sir Alec Martin*

127. SCENE AT SANDBATH

John Leech   *Sir Alec Martin*

ductions will be found to stand higher than might have been anticipated even in the scale of European nineteenth-century painting. It would be futile to mention with it the real French painters of the time; but, at least, there is nothing to compare with it in Germany, in Austria, or Spain, or Italy, or the Netherlands, at that time.

The qualities of this school, taken as a whole, consist largely, it must be confessed, in period interest. But all eighteenth-century paintings, save those of the very best artists of the time, rely also upon this fictitious charm. A Longhi or a Laroon have the same appeal as that painting by W. M. Egley, or the nearly synonymous Augustus Egg. In technique there is little or nothing to choose between them, while these later works have, it is certain, a more solid accomplishment behind them. An exhibition of inferior French eighteenth-century paintings, with too much of Lancret and Pater and of the lesser men, cannot last in the memory as did those pictures collected together for the Victorian Exhibition at the Leicester Galleries in the summer of 1937. That consisted almost entirely of half-forgotten names. The best painter shown, there is little doubt, was A. Boyd Houghton, better known for his woodcut illustrations to books of the 'sixties, and in particular for his *Arabian Nights*. Boyd Houghton was short-lived, dying at about forty years of age, and in his busy life he can have found but little time to practise painting. The exhibition contained one picture by his hand, called by the sentimental title of Baby. It was a study of an infant lying in a cradle, watched over by its mother. In the background, a glass-fronted cupboard or bookcase contained the reflection of a bearded face, in all probability that of the painter. This description may not sound as if it could constitute a work of art, but the picture had the quality of the finest Walter Sickert, with, as well, that period value which is now beginning to enhance the works of that greatest of our living painters. One or two other small paintings by Boyd Houghton were also shown, but they had not quite the quality of that described. For, in its way, this could not be bettered. Nor is it easy to detect the influences that went to the making of it. This painting has no traces of French influence; neither is it akin to the Dutch painters of interiors. Even as to its English origins there can be considerable doubts; neither Turner, Constable, Wilkie, Etty, nor Lawrence are hinted at. It would seem as if this little picture was produced upon entirely independent lines, in common with the rest of the lesser or unconscious Pre-Raphaelites. But Boyd Houghton, it must be urged, has none of the near-absurdity of Augustus Egg; he was a supremely competent draughtsman, as can be seen in his woodcut illustrations; and, in the rare moments when he painted, his is never the hand of the amateur. Boyd Houghton was condemned by circumstances to waste his time and energies upon means that were below the level of his talents. He had the makings of a considerable minor painter, but was seldom given the opportunity to exercise them.

John Leech, though with a different orientation, is another case in point. As with so many novels, his story only really begins when it is ended. He is known to the world for his coloured drawings to the novels of Surtees. It would be invidious to pretend that Leech did not enjoy this phase of his work; it is contradicted by the drawings themselves. His other main activity was the production of drawings, by the hundred, for *Punch*. These are invariably excellent; and in spare moments he drew for other books. Admirers of Leech will find one of his most admirable works in the coloured folding frontispiece for the description of his journey to Ireland with Dean Hole. It is a drawing of the fisher-girls of the Claddagh, at Galway, and Leech can be seen in this approaching nearer to his final development.

For many years Leech drew the coloured supplements to *Punch's Almanack*, an annual publication which must have circulated in tens of thousands. The Scene at Sandbath (127), of which an illustration is given, is one of his original coloured drawings from which the plates for the Almanack were made. It is a very large drawing, beautifully clear and simple in colour and in design, and full of humour. Those extraordinary small children of the period are wonderfully observed; the girl in the crinoline walking the plank is a delightful touch; while the young girl standing on the left, in a black cap, long blonde hair falling to her waist, and a cloak, will win every heart. The early steamer, or it does not even appear to be a steamer, completes this vision of dead summers.

About the year 1858, Leech, who had always been ambitious to become a painter, began to make the enlargement in oil-colours of what he considered to be the best of his drawings for *Punch*. These were exhibited, with much diffidence on the part of the artist, at the Egyptian Hall in 1863, only a year before his premature death. He was, in fact, only forty-seven years of age. The fate of these oil-sketches has been very obscure; for though some fifty to sixty of them were shown, it is but rarely that they come to light. Scarborough Sands (126) is the only one of them known to the writer. Unfortunately, owing to the scale of reproduction, it is difficult to see the surpassing merits of this work. For it is a wonderful and exceptional thing. The grey sky alone is an extraordinary piece of work, with its impression of a north-easter blowing, which is borne out by the billowing dresses. The sea, too, is most accurately rendered, as can be vouched for

James Tissot   129.   THE BALL ON SHIPBOARD

by the writer, who had this same stretch of sand before his eyes during the most impressionable years of childhood. The figures in this sketch in oils are almost miracles of observation. Nowhere else can we see and know exactly how a fashionable crowd would appear in the buffetings of a strong wind. This can be looked at indefinitely, and there are always new discoveries to be made. The clothes, in themselves, are of extreme interest. These are the fashionable persons of London, or the rich landowners and their families of Yorkshire. Their ancestors may have been visiting the same northern watering-place for as much as a century before this, so long had it been famous as a resort. There is so much to point out in this picture. The man with a telescope under his arm, standing in the foreground with his back to us; the two women in crinolines that lift into the air and reveal their black kid boots and white stockings; the volunteer officer and his friend who are regarding them; a further group of a cloaked woman walking away from us, head down in the wind; a Dundreary-like, whiskered and bowlered man, in a check suit with a crinoline, so to speak, on his arm; the old fisherman, or lifeboatman, on the left; the innumerable children and crinolines and bathing machines in the distance; or that fascinating view of the harbour, with the salt wind and, almost, the harbour smell, the tar and ropes, and herring-salting in the air.

This oil-sketch must date from 1858-59, two years during which it is known that Leech spent his summer holiday at Scarborough. More than one search through the files of *Punch* has failed to reveal the original drawing from which this is said to be taken. Instead, it has brought to light at least two more drawings of the scene; one, a sudden squall of rain, high up in the town near the Castle hill, and the sudden way in which it dispersed this same fashionable crowd in crinolines with their escorts of check suits, whiskers, and top-hats; the other, a drawing also, of the sands, with an immense crowd containing literally dozens of figures, and, in the foreground, what may be the only appearance in art of a Skye terrier, that typical product of the Victorian Highlands; with its echoes of turreted Balmoral, carpets and curtains of tartan, and the little Prince Imperial dressed by his mother in a kilt. The same drawing, too, contains the only image in art of the delightful open pony carriages that were peculiar to Scarborough. A boy, dressed in white breeches and a brightly coloured jockey's shirt and cap, rode, postilion, on the pony and drove the carriage. It is such echoes, or suggestions, that are implicit in the painting, too.

This little sketch in oils, which is something transcendental and apart from anything else described in this book, reveals Leech to us as beginning his true career just in the very end of his days. It would be of absorbing interest to see more of his pictures from that exhibition at the Egyptian Hall and to know how high a place was occupied by this particular example. This tentative effort on the part of Leech might have begun a whole new chapter in painting. His touch, which is competent and entirely reliable in drawing, takes on, in painting, an altogether new direction and potency. This is like a Japanese scroll-painting of the Heian period, when the *Tale of Genji* was written. It has that fantastic elegance and improbability. Perhaps the 'sixties, that most far-fetched of periods in European costume, might have found its supreme commentator in this painter who died too soon.

Those artists who illustrated the woodcut books of the 'sixties were so tied down to their tasks that it required much strength of purpose to embark upon any other project. We have noticed this in the case of Boyd Houghton and, if Leech was just as laboriously employed, the same thing is true of all the others who contributed to this great period in book illustration. Pinwell, for example, a most graceful and delicate little master, after his fashion, seems to have succumbed to hard work and too persistent effort. It is true, also, of the consumptive Frederick Walker, who had yet the energy to embark upon large oil paintings. These were greeted with every success in their day; now, they are in that same limbo in which his contemporary Fortuny is to be found. But the water-colour drawings of Frederick Walker have a different and a better appeal. Spring (125) is a particular favourite among these. It is a drawing of two children picking primroses in a coppice. The woods are not yet green and it must be early April, just before the leaves. This, again, is a drawing of pure sentiment. It has no period interest, unless we wonder whether the little boy and girl can still be alive. Volunteers at the Firing-Point (128), by H. T. Wells, on the other hand, is a complete period piece. It must date from just after the great Volunteer movement of 1859. The white veils worn by some of the Volunteers round their hats, relates this picture, by reminiscence, to Frith's Derby Day. There is something, perhaps, a little trying to modern eyes in the physiognomy of some of the Volunteers, noticeably in the man on horseback and in the Gladstonian old man at the right. The Garibaldian influence is to be discerned in the tall, bearded figure standing with his back to us. This, in fact, is not a picture at all; it could all have been done equally well with the camera. And yet it is of interest, if from this one point only, that a modern group of this calibre would not be nearly so well executed. No one now has the necessary patience and industry to consume himself and his time in a picture of this nature.

But this book can end, or nearly so, with the consideration of someone who was indisputably among the lesser masters. This is James Tissot, who has lately been brought back into popularity by the two comprehensive exhibitions of his work at the Leicester Galleries. It is easy to overpraise him; and as facile to deny him what is his just due. A prominent contemporary painter has compared him, in the public press, to Vermeer of Delft; while more imposing critics have stated their horror of his paintings in such terms that they recoil from any further mention of them. He is, in fact, anathema to the strictly contemporary taste and an unalloyed pleasure to those who do not take their delights too seriously. The truth is that Tissot was a truthful and unimaginative Frenchman, properly trained and not afraid of stating his own convictions. But he is also to some extent of romantic import. Although his height of fame was only in the 'seventies, for he settled in London after the Franco-Prussian War, and in spite of the fact that his pictures sold for sums which all modern painters would envy, all that is to do with him is shrouded in the obscurity that hides every generation from that of its grandparents. He left London in 1882 or 1883, owing to the effects of some sentimental crisis in his life. After living a short time in Paris he then undertook his illustrations to the Bible, which involved him in journeys to the Holy Land and occupied the remainder of his days. He died in 1903, in a religious retreat.

Such are the bare outlines of his life. But the fascination of Tissot lies in the nearly impenetrable mists that surround him. The same young and beautiful woman who appears in so many of his paintings, and generally, as in The Last Evening (130), with the figure of the artist himself gazing deeply at her, or in conversation with her, this, together with other mysterious features in his career, have shed a halo of romance round him. There were rumours of a suicide, though these are now dispelled by the discovery of the lady's grave, for she was, in reality, married to the artist just before her death. It is to be imagined that, being a staunch Catholic, he had been prevented from marrying her until she was on her deathbed. Certainly an atmosphere of intense romantic devotion distils itself from his many renderings of her face and form, some of them cleverly differentiated, so that identification is never absolutely certain. She is usually in association, too, with other stock types or models of the painter, such as the stout, bearded naval officer who appears in The Last Evening.

Tissot, as Mr. James Laver points out in his excellent little book upon him, was a native of the French seaport, Nantes, and this gave him a love of shipping and an experienced eye at the delineation of their intricate rigging, for the steamboats of the 'sixties and 'seventies still relied partly upon sail. In The Last Evening there is an absolute forest of masts and ropes, all painted with masterly precision and, we may be certain, with entire accuracy. This is a good example of Tissot's art. The figure of the woman is carried out with an immense competence, and Tissot, who took a manifest delight in feminine fashions, has excelled himself with her plaid cape and with the tartan rug that covers her knees. Her head and clasped hands, and the tender expression of her features, are beautifully rendered. Tissot himself, it must be, leans forward towards her, entirely absorbed in his contemplation of her.

Entre les deux mon cœur balance (131) is less spectacular as a painting. The interest centres nearly entirely upon the young woman who talks to the soldier. It is only her figure that redeems the picture from the common-place. Her companion is silent and at a disadvantage. The soldier, who again is a slightly changed figure of the painter himself, pays no attention to her. He concentrates his attention upon the first young woman. She is dressed in a black and white striped dress, with delightful frilled cuffs, and a plaid rug over her arm. In her other hand she holds her folded parasol coquettishly in the air. Her curls of hair and nose and eyebrows are painted in the most attractive manner, and this figure of her, though it differs in colour, for her hair is not blonde, must convey his feeling, at least, of a conversation with the woman whom he loved.

The Ball on Shipboard (129) is an altogether more important painting. It is said to represent a dance given on board the Royal yacht (the *Victoria and Albert*?), during Cowes week in 1873. There has been much conjecture as to the persons represented, for there can be no doubt that they are all portraits. Queen Alexandra, then Princess of Wales, has been suggested for the young woman standing by the companion-way, wearing a sailor straw hat tilted up upon her forehead. The old gentleman next to her may be the Czar Alexander II; or it might be Lord Londonderry. The charming young girl in the left foreground, looking out of the picture towards the spectator, has not been identified; neither has her companion sitting next to her. Delightful passages in this picture are the young girl hurrying up the companion-way, who looks down, behind her, at the dance in progress on the lower deck; the immensely tall bearded man talking to a woman on the far side of the stairway; and the group of four women talking to a man near the deck rail. Two of these women hold fans; and all four are deep in an animated conversation. The ceiling is one gay mass of bunting and flags; while the presence, in their patterns, of so many crowned and double-headed eagles suggests that it was the Czar in whose honour the dance was given. The young woman who stands talking to the Princess of Wales and to the Czar may be taken as the epitome of feminine fashion

130. THE LAST EVENING

James Tissot   *The Guildhall Art Gallery*

131. "ENTRE LES DEUX MON CŒUR BALANCE . . ."

James Tissot   *The Leicester Galleries*

132. HAMMERSMITH BRIDGE ON BOAT-RACE DAY

Walter Greaves

The Tate Gallery

133. LAWRENCE STREET, CHELSEA

Walter Greaves

Mrs. Marchant

in the 'seventies. In her figure can be seen in what lay the contemporary fascination; for no photograph can tell us of this, and the mere fashion-plates of the time are grotesque and remote, conveying nothing of the true appearance of a beautiful woman at that epoch. It is to be noted that this painting dates from so early a year in the 'seventies that the crinoline has not quite disappeared, while the bustle, which was so characteristic of the 'eighties, has not yet made its appearance. This painting must be, in every respect, the best picture of social life of the time. The rendering of every detail is beautifully and pleasurably accurate; a shawl and bonnet and a parasol, for instance, upon an empty chair in the foreground, have even the touch of Degas, who was the fellow-student and friend of Tissot.

The general level of his paintings is consistently good to those, that is to say, who are not disturbed by his complacency and by his willingness, among other instances of this kind, to paint a hansom-cab as the centre of a whole picture. Of this there is a conspicuous example in one particular painting by his hand. The Ball on Shipboard, then, has its equal in at least several other pictures by Tissot. He was, as well, a good portrait painter. His group of the Empress Eugénie and the Prince Imperial, taken in the grounds of Chislehurst, and now in the Louvre, is more than a mere historical document. It was only a few years since Winterhalter had painted the Empress in the midst of the ladies of her Court, in those floating dresses and wide flopping hats under the summer trees. Since then the disaster of Sedan had come. In her portrait by Tissot she is to be seen on the arm of the Prince Imperial, Napoleon IV as he might have been, among the fallen red leaves of a patch of garden. It is the only good portrait of the Prince Imperial as a young man. Another fine Tissot is his portrait of Colonel Burnaby, the hero of *A Ride to Khiva*, who was soon to be slain at Tel-el-Kebir by the Dervish spears. The great height of Burnaby is cleverly shown, although he is seated in the picture, and splendid play is made with his helmet and breastplate lying beside him. This portrait is agreeably unlike the Millais or Herkomer which was the custom at the time.

It is extremely improbable that any painter will ever again address himself to the problems of Tissot. The film has killed direct representation; and Tissot, as a painter, had ever the equivalent of the old-fashioned photographer's black hood over his head. His paintings, that is to say, are immensely long exposures of the everyday scene. He painted nothing that the camera could not catch. His actual brushwork is level and smooth; never hurried nor impetuous. Everyday life quite contented him. There is little or no influence of any other painter in his work; a suggestion, it

93

may be, of the Belgian Alfred Stevens, and just a hint, and no more, of Degas, whose picture of The Cotton Exchange at New Orleans must certainly have appeared to Tissot, if he knew it, as a masterpiece in that kind of painting to which he aspired himself. There is no sign, certainly, of any English influence in Tissot. But his best works are pictures of English life, by a hand which it does not take long to identify as that of a Frenchman. As paintings they are skilfully representative and utterly unimaginative. But the truth, and not fiction, is what is required of pure executants, whether in music or in the fine arts. Tissot certainly was truthful; and, in the light of that, it is easy to find endless enjoyment in his pictures of that far-off age, so remote from us just because it is so near. The details of dresses; the sheer delight in the webs of rope and rigging; the recurrence even of that same mysterious and beautiful woman; the attempts to discover an identity for persons who were alive so short a time ago; these are some of the things which may keep living the fame of Tissot, who, in comparison with our own contemporary painters of fact, was a master to be spoken of with respect. Tissot was utterly and entirely the painter of his age and, as such, his like can never be born again.

Last of all, we reach the close of this book with a mysterious figure, Walter Greaves. This man and his brother, who lived as young men in Chelsea, early came into contact with Whistler. They rowed him in a boat upon the Thames, helped him prepare his colours, and acted as general agents or servants for him. Soon Walter Greaves became dignified into what was nearly the assistant of Whistler. He was an eccentric character who lived into extreme old age, only dying in 1931, and his mode of life and oddness of temperament make a correct view of him most difficult to secure. His portrait of his sister is very nearly a wonderful picture. Lawrence Street, Chelsea (133), is typical of his paintings of Chelsea, done in considerable numbers. Hammersmith Bridge on Boat-race Day (132), in the Tate Gallery, is his masterpiece. This is the work of a naif, and has the quality and merits of a painting by the Douanier Rousseau. In fact, in midst of the Victorian seriousness Walter Greaves has achieved a fantasy, pure and simple, but brought about by his pleasant lack of professional skill. The perspective of his bridge tails away into the future, towards all the unrepresentative or abstract fantasies that are still to come. He points out of the nineteenth century into the twentieth. This fact by itself is sufficient praise for him; but it need not be, equally and conversely, the blame for those whose conventions tied them entirely to their own times. This may be, and often is, as in the case of Tissot, their message to the generations that are to come.

NOTES ON THE ILLUSTRATIONS

By MICHAEL SEVIER

MILLAIS, SIR JOHN EVERETT, P.R.A. (1829–1896)

1. THE BLIND GIRL. Oil on canvas, 31¾×21 inches.

The first conception of the picture came to the artist in 1854. J. G. Millais, his son and biographer, states that the landscape motif was first discovered at Icklesham near Winchelsea, but finished at Barnhill, outside Perth, where Millais also found the models for the figures. Sir Sydney Cockerell, on the other hand, says that ' The background consists of a view of Winchelsea as seen from the flat marshland to the east, and is so accurate that every building and nearly every tree can still be recognised.' The birds and animals were all painted from nature, as well as the butterfly, which was especially captured for the purpose. Not knowing that a second rainbow is merely a reflection of the first, Millais did not originally reverse the order of the colours—a mistake which he later corrected.

Signed and dated : *Millais*, 1856.

First exhibited at the Royal Academy in 1856, and awarded the prize of the Liverpool Academy in 1858.

Former owners : J. Miller, Preston (sold at Christie's in 1858 for £315 ; Roberts ; W. Graham ; Albert Wood, Conway ; William Kenrick, who presented the picture to the Gallery in 1892.

Coll. : *City of Birmingham Art Gallery.*

HOGARTH, WILLIAM (1697–1764)

2. NOON. Oil on canvas, 24×29 inches.

' Noon ' belongs to a set of four paintings entitled ' The Four Times of the Day,' which were painted in 1738. The set was engraved by Hogarth, and published in the same year.

The crying boy is said to have been sketched by Hogarth from a figure in Poussin's ' The Rape of the Sabines,' which was in the possession of Mr. Hoare at Stourhead.

' Noon ' was bought at the sale which Hogarth held at his house in Leicester Fields during February 1745 for 37 guineas by the Earl of Ancaster.

Coll. : *Earl of Ancaster, Grimsthorpe Castle, Lincolnshire.*

3. THE DISTRESSED POET. Oil on canvas, 25×30⅞ inches.

Under the first-state engraving of this picture appears the following quotation from the *Dunciad* :

> ' Studious he sate, with all his books around,
> Sinking, from thought to thought, a vast profound !
> Plung'd for his sense, but found no bottom there,
> Then writ, and flounder'd on, in mere despair.'

It must therefore be assumed that the subject was inspired by the plight of the poet Lewis Theobald, described by Pope in his poem. The picture which hangs on the wall above the figure of the poet is said to represent Pope thrashing the bookseller Curle.

Signed and dated : *W. Hogarth*, 1735.

Engraved by Hogarth, and published, first state in 1736, second state in 1740.

The picture was given by the artist to Mrs. Draper, Queen Caroline's midwife. At her death it was sold for five guineas to a solicitor called Ward, and at the latter's sale purchased for fourteen guineas by the first Earl Grosvenor.

Presented to the Gallery by Sir Charles Hyde in 1934.

Coll. : *City of Birmingham Art Gallery.*

4. THE GATE OF CALAIS. Oil on canvas, 31¼ × 37¼ inches.

Hogarth went to France in 1748 and, according to Walpole (letter to Sir Horace Mann of 15th December 1748), when making a sketch of the drawbridge at Calais, ' was seized and carried to the Governor, where he was forced to prove his vocation by producing several *caricatures* of the French; particularly a scene of the shore, with an immense piece of beef landing for the Lion d'Argent, the English inn at Calais, and several hungry friars following it. They were much diverted with his drawings and dismissed him.' Hogarth himself refers to the incident and the picture that ensued as follows : ' As I was sauntering about . . . near the Gate, which it seems was built by the English when the place was in our possession, I remarked some appearance of the arms of *England* on the front. By this idle curiosity, I was prompted to make a sketch of it, which being observed, I was taken into custody; but not attempting to conceal any of my sketches or memorandums, which were found to be merely those of a painter for his private use, without any relation to fortification . . . I was only closely confined to my own lodgings, till the wind changed *for England* : when I no sooner arrived, than I set about the picture ; made the gate my background ; and in one corner introduced my own portrait, which has generally been thought a correct likeness, with the soldier's hand upon my shoulder. By the fat friar, who stops the lean cook that is sinking under the weight of a vast sirloin of beef, and two of *the military* bearing off a great kettle of *soup maigre*, I meant to display to my own countrymen the striking difference between the food, priests, soldiers, etc., of two nations so contiguous that in a clear day one coast may be seen from the other. The melancholy and miserable Highlander, browsing on his scanty fare, consisting of a bit of bread and an onion, is intended for one of the many that fled from this country after the rebellion ' (cf. John Ireland, *Hogarth Illustrated*).

The ' fat friar ' is a portrait of the engraver, John Pine.

Engraved by Hogarth with the title ' Roast Beef of old England,' and published in 1749.

Exhibited at the ' Society of Arts ' in Spring Gardens in 1761.

Former collections : bought from the artist by the first Earl of Charlemont ; H. W. Bolckow ; Agnew ; Duke of Westminster, who presented the picture to the nation in 1895.

Coll. : *The National Gallery, London.*

ZOFFANY, JOHN, R.A. (1733–1810)

5. THE LAPIDARIES. Oil on canvas, 35½ × 27½ inches.

A portrait of Peter Dollond, the King's optician, and his attendant.

Exhibited at the Royal Academy in 1772 under the title 'An Optician with his Attendant.' Walpole wrote about the picture : ' Extremely natural, but the characters too common nature and the chiaroscuro destroyed by his servility in imitating the reflexions of the glass.'

Coll. : *His Majesty the King, Windsor Castle.*

6. CONCERT OF WANDERING MINSTRELS. Oil on panel, 14½ × 18 inches.

Painted in Italy in 1772 or 1773 for the Duke Ferdinand of Bourbon. Formerly entitled, with no justification, 'Blind Minstrels.'

Coll. : *The Picture Gallery, Parma.*

FÜSSLI, JOHANN HEINRICH, KNOWN AS FUSELI, HENRY, R.A. (1741–1825)

7. THE TOILET. Pencil and wash drawing, touched with water-colour, 17½ × 11½ inches.

The same three figures, though differing in detail, appear in a four-figure composition in oil, which is now in the possession of Professor Ganz, Basle, and which was engraved by Rhodes as an illustration to William Cowper's poem ' The Progress of Error.' The Engraving was published in 1807 with the following quotation from the poem :

' Folly ever has a vacant stare,
A simpering countenance, and a trifling air ;
But innocence, sedate, serene, erect,
Delights us, by engaging our respect.'

It is the figure of innocence which is missing in the present drawing.

Former collections : Dr. John Percy ; Herbert ; Horne ; Sir Edward Marsh.

Coll. : *Brinsley Ford, Esq., London.*

NOTES ON THE ILLUSTRATIONS

CRUIKSHANK, GEORGE (1792–1878)

8. THE RUNAWAY KNOCK. Oil on panel, 24×19½ inches.

Pasted on the back of the panel is the following receipt: ' London, June 18th, 1855. Recd. Joseph Robinson, Esq., the sum of One Hundred pounds for a picture entitled " A Runaway Knock " (Frame included), reserving the copyright. Geo. Cruikshank.'
Exhibited at the British Institution in 1855.
Coll. : *W. T. Spencer, Esq., London.*

HUNT, WILLIAM HOLMAN (1827–1910)

9. MAY MORNING ON MAGDALEN TOWER. Oil on canvas, 59½×78 inches.

The ceremony depicted is celebrated each year on 1st May at sunrise on the tower of Magdalen College, Oxford. It is a floral festival which is believed to be of Roman or Druidic origin but has now acquired a Christian significance, being held in honour of St. Mary the Virgin and St. Mary Magdalen. The flowers used on the occasion are gathered on a meadow where, according to tradition, they were originally planted by the Crusaders, who brought them back from Palestine.
In his picture Holman Hunt did not strictly adhere to reality, as he himself stated in a letter to Mr. and Mrs. Cadbury. ' I ought to say,' he wrote, ' that my treatment of the ceremony is rather abstract than of prosaic fact, inasmuch as on May mornings nowadays half the tower is crowded by undergraduates waiting the termination of the hymn to engage in youthful frolic. This having nothing to do with the vital ceremony, I used an artistic licence to remove these playful intruders, together with an unsightly rail which, in fact, separates the two groups.' The picture, which was painted in 1899, was first conceived in 1888, when for many weeks on end Hunt ascended at sunrise to the roof of the College and worked there on the smaller version of the subject, which is now at the Birmingham Art Gallery. The figures were painted from life and many of them represent dignitaries and choristers of the College. Their names appear on a key below the picture. The silver bowl in the foreground is the oldest piece of plate belonging to the College, and dates from the reign of William III.
Purchased from Mrs. Holman Hunt in 1919.
Coll. : *The Lady Lever Art Gallery, Port Sunlight.*

10. THE HIRELING SHEPHERD. Oil on canvas, 29¾×42 inches.

The greater part of the picture was painted at Ewell in 1851. It was exhibited in the same year at the Royal Academy, the following quotation from *King Lear* accompanying the title in the catalogue : ' Sleepest or wakest thou, jolly shepherd ? Thy sheep be in the corn ; and, for one blast of thy minikin mouth, thy sheep shall take no harm.' Another version of the same subject, different in some details, is in the possession of Sir George Agnew.
Signed and dated : *Holman Hunt, 1851, Ewell.*
Bought from the artist in 1851 by James Leathart. Purchased by the Gallery in 1896.
Coll. : *Manchester City Art Gallery.*

BROWN, FORD MADOX (1821–1893)

11. WORK. Oil on canvas, 54½×77½ inches.

F. M. Hueffer gives in his biography of F. M. Brown the artist's own detailed description of ' Work ' of which the following is an abbreviated transcript :
' This picture was begun in 1852 at Hampstead. The background, which represents the main street of that suburb not far from the Heath, was painted on the spot. At the time extensive excavations were going on in the neighbourhood, and, seeing and studying daily as I did the British excavator, or *navvy*, as he designates himself, in the full swing of his activity . . . it appeared to me that he was at least as worthy of the powers of an English painter as the fisherman of the Adriatic, the peasant of the Campagne, or the Neapolitan lazzarone. Gradually this idea developed itself into that of *Work* as it now exists, with the British excavator for a central group, as the outward and visible type of *Work*. Here are presented the young navvy in the pride of

97

manly health and beauty ; the strong fully developed navvy who does his work and loves his beer ; the selfish old bachelor navvy, stout of limb, and perhaps a trifle tough in those regions where compassion is said to reside ; the navvy of strong animal nature, who, but that he was when young *taught* to work at useful work, might even now be working at the *useless crank*. Then Paddy with his lorry and his pipe in his mouth. . . . Next in value of significance to these is the ragged wretch who has never been *taught* to *work*. . . . But for a certain effeminate gentleness of disposition and a love of nature he might have been a burglar ! . . . In the very opposite scale from the man who can't work, at the further corner of the picture, are two men who appear to have nothing to do. These are the brain-workers, who, seeming to be idle, work and are the cause of well-ordained work and happiness in others. . . . Next to these, on the shaded bank, are different characters out of work : haymakers in quest of employment ; a Stoic from the Emerald Island . . . a young shoeless Irishman, with his wife, feeding their first-born with cold pap ; an old sailor turned haymaker ; and two young peasants. . . . Behind the Pariah, who has never learned to work, appears a group of a very different class, who, from an opposite cause, have not been sufficiently used to work either. These are the *rich*, who " have no need to work "—not at least for bread. . . . The pastry-cook's tray, the symbol of superfluity, accompanies these. It is peculiarly English ; I never saw it abroad that I remember. . . . Past the pastry-cook's tray come two married ladies. The elder and more serious of the two devotes her energies to tract distributing, and has just flung one entitled " The Hodman's Haven ; or, Drink for Thirsty Souls " to the somewhat uncompromising specimen of navvy humanity descending the ladder. . . . In front of her is the lady whose only business in life as yet is to dress and look beautiful for our benefit. . . . Would anyone wish it otherwise ? Certainly not I, dear lady. Only in your own interest . . . I would beg to call your attention to my group of small, exceedingly ragged, dirty children in the foreground of my picture. That they are motherless the baby's black ribbons and their extreme dilapidation indicate, making them all the more worthy of consideration. . . . The dog which accompanies them is evidently of the same outcast sort as themselves . . . rugged democrat as he is, he is gentle to them, only he hates minions of aristocracy in red jackets. The old bachelor navvy's small valuable bull-pup also instinctively distrusts outlandish-looking dogs in jackets.

' The couple on horseback in the middle distance consists of a gentleman, still young, and his daughter. This gentleman is evidently very rich, probably a colonel in the army, with a seat in Parliament, and fifteen thousand a year and a pack of hounds . . . and could he only be got to hear what the two sages in the corner have to say, I have no doubt he would be easily won over. But the road is blocked, and the daughter says we must go back, papa, round the other way.

' The man with the beer-tray, calling " Beer ho ! " so lustily, is a specimen of town pluck and energy contrasted with country thews and sinews. . . . On the wall are posters and bills, one of the " Boys' Home, 41 Euston Road " . . . one of " The Working Men's College, Great Ormond Street," or if you object to these, then a police bill offering 50s. reward in a matter of highway robbery. Back in the distance we see the Assembly Room of the " Flamstead Institute of Arts," where Professor Snoox is about to repeat his interesting lecture on the habits of the domestic cat. . . . The less important characters in the background require little comment. . . .

' *N.B.*—In several cases I have had the advantage of sittings from personages of note. . . . As my object, however, in all cases, is to delineate types and not individuals, and as, moreover, I never contemplated employing their renown to benefit my own reputation, I refrain from publishing their names.' (Cf. Ford M. Hueffer, *Ford Madox Brown*, 1896, pp. 189–195.)

The sitters whose names are known include Thomas Carlyle and the Rev. Frederick Denison Maurice (the two ' brain-workers '), the artist's wife (the lady behind the flower-girl), Arthur Gabriel Madox Brown (the baby in the girl's arms), and R. B. Martineau (the gentleman on horseback).

Though the picture was started in 1852, it was put aside until 1856, when T. E. Plint commissioned Brown to finish it. This took the artist several years to accomplish.

Signed and dated : *F. Madox Brown, 1852–65*.

A smaller version of the subject, commissioned by J. Leathart, is now in the City of Birmingham Art Gallery. A sketch for the background belonged (in 1896) to Mrs. Thomas Woolner and a pen-and-ink drawing, executed in 1860, to T. E. Plint.

Bought by the Gallery from T. E. Plint in 1885.

Coll. : *Manchester City Art Gallery*.

12. PRETTY BAA LAMBS. Oil on panel, 7¾ × 10 inches.

A small replica of a picture painted in the summer of 1851 at Stockwell and Clapham Common.

The present work was produced in 1852–53 in Thomas Seddon's studio in London, and was first exhibited at the ' Sketch Exhibition ' in 1853. It was bought from the artist for five pounds by B. G. Windus in 1855.
Signed and dated : *F. Madox Brown*, 52.
Purchased for the Museum out of the Magdalen College Fund in 1909.
Coll. : *The Ashmolean Museum, Oxford.*

BRETT, JOHN, A.R.A. (1830–1902)

13. THE STONEBREAKER. Oil on canvas, 19½ × 26½ inches.

The hill in the distance is Box Hill. The inscription on the milestone reads: 'London 23.'
Signed and dated : *John Brett*, 1857–58.
Exhibited at the Royal Academy in 1858.
Bequeathed to the Gallery by Mrs. Sarah Ann Barrow in 1918.
Coll. : *The Walker Art Gallery, Liverpool.*

ROWLANDSON, THOMAS (1756–1827)

14. THE EXHIBITION ' STARECASE.' Pen and wash, 15½ × 10⅜ inches.

Also known as ' A Soirée at the Royal Academy.' The staircase is in Somerset House, where the exhibitions of the Royal Academy were held from 1780 to 1837. An etching of the drawing was published about 1800.
Formerly owned by the late Henry Tonks, who bequeathed it to University College.
Coll. : *University College, London.*

15. THE UNLUCKY GAMBLER. Water-colour, 6¾ × 4¾ inches.

The gambler is seen leaving Phillips' gambling-house. Another water-colour by Rowlandson in the same collection, representing Phillips and his wife, bears, probably in the artist's own handwriting, the inscription : ' Phillips, commonly called the God of the Greeks, and his Rib.'
Inscribed: *T. Rowlandson.*
Coll. : *Henry Reitlinger, Esq., London.*

16. VISIT TO AN OLD ACQUAINTANCE. Water-colour, 14¾ × 11¼ inches.

Signed and dated : *Rowlandson*, 1819.
Coll. : *Henry Reitlinger, Esq., London.*

17. THE RETURN. Pen and water-colour, 15 × 19½ inches.

Signed and dated : *Rowlandson*, 1787.
Engraved in 1788.
Formerly in the collection of Lord Carnarvon.
Coll. : *J. Leslie Wright, Esq., Warwick.*

18. DRESSING FOR THE MASQUERADE. Water-colour, 11½ × 15¾ inches.

Inscribed : *Rowlandson.*
Coll. : *Sir Edward Marsh, London.*

19. THE GARDENER'S OFFERING. Water-colour, 11 × 16¾ inches.

Coll. : *Henry Harris, Esq., London.*

LAMI, LOUIS EUGÈNE (1800–1890)

20. SCENE IN BELGRAVE SQUARE ; LADIES ENTERING THEIR CARRIAGE. Water-colour, 5 × 9 inches.

Signed : *Eugène Lami.*
Presented to the Museum by F. R. Bryan in 1880.
Coll. : *Victoria and Albert Museum, London.*

21. SCENE AT LUDGATE CIRCUS. Water-colour, $5\frac{1}{2}\times9\frac{1}{2}$ inches.

Signed and dated : *E. L.*, 1850.
Presented to the Museum by F. R. Bryan in 1880.
Coll. : *Victoria and Albert Museum, London.*

EGLEY, W. MAW
(Exhibited at the Royal Academy between 1843 and 1893)

22. THE INTERIOR OF A BUS. Oil on panel, $16\frac{1}{2}\times15\frac{3}{4}$ inches.

Signed and dated : *W. Maw Egley*, 1859.
Exhibited in 1859 at the British Institution with the title ' Omnibus Life in London.'
Formerly in the collection of the late Mr. Hugh Blaker. Now on loan at the Tate Gallery.
Coll. : *Miss Blaker, London.*

HICKS, GEORGE ELGAR
(Exhibited at the Royal Academy from 1848 to 1903)

23. DIVIDEND DAY AT THE BANK OF ENGLAND. Oil on canvas, $9\frac{3}{4}\times14\frac{1}{2}$ inches.

Signed and dated : *G. Hicks*, 1859.
Exhibited at the Royal Academy in 1859.
Coll. : *The Leicester Galleries, London.*

UNIDENTIFIED ARTIST (*c.* 1868)

24. THE LOWTHER ARCADE. Oil on canvas, $23\times32\frac{1}{2}$ inches.

The Lowther Arcade led from the Strand to St. Martin's Churchyard ; its site is now occupied by Coutts Bank. It was designed in 1830–32 by William Young and built by Herbert. Lord Lowther (1787–1872), after whom the Arcade was named, was Chief Commissioner of Woods and Forests at the time of its erection.
Coll. : *The Leicester Galleries, London.*

HOGARTH, WILLIAM (1697–1764)
MARRIAGE À LA MODE

Figures 25, 26 and 27 are respectively scene 1, scene 2 and scene 6 of the ' pictorial drama,' consisting of six paintings, entitled ' Marriage à la Mode.' The series was completed in 1744 and engraved ' by the best masters in Paris ' : G. Scotin, B. Baron and F. S. Ravenet. They were exhibited by Hogarth at his house, the Golden Head, and at Cock's Auction Rooms, but found no purchaser. Five years after their production, on 12th June 1751, Hogarth disposed of them by private auction for 120 guineas. They were bought by John Lane, of Hillingden, near Uxbridge, who was the only bidder. Lane bequeathed the pictures to his nephew, Colonel J. F. Cawthorne, who put them up for sale in 1792 and 1796. They failed on both occasions to realise the reserve price and were eventually sold in 1797 for 1000 guineas to J. J. Angerstein. With the rest of the Angerstein collection they were acquired by the nation in 1824.
Coll. : *The Tate Gallery, Millbank, London.*

25. THE MARRIAGE CONTRACT. Oil on canvas, 28×36 inches.

Engraved by G. Scotin, and published in 1745.

26. THE BREAKFAST SCENE. Oil on canvas, 28×36 inches.

Austin Dobson (cf. his *William Hogarth*) states that according to the late Lord Houghton the room represents the drawing-room at 24 Arlington Street, the one-time domicile of Horace Walpole. Francis Hayman is supposed to have been the model for the figure of the husband.
Engraved by B. Baron, and published in 1745.

27. THE DEATH OF THE COUNTESS. Oil on canvas, 28×36 inches.

The view through the window is of London Bridge.
Engraved by G. Scotin, and published in 1745.

NOTES ON THE ILLUSTRATIONS

THE RAKE'S PROGRESS

Figures 28, 29 and 30 are respectively the eighth, second and third of the set of eight paintings known as 'The Rake's Progress.' The set was painted in 1735 at Isleworth, where Hogarth then temporarily resided, and was engraved by him, and published in the same year. Hogarth originally sold the eight pictures at the private sale which he held in 1745 (see note on figure 2) for 176 guineas to Alderman Beckford, of Fonthill. They were later acquired by Colonel Fullarton for £872, 10s., and purchased at his sale in 1802 for 570 guineas by Mr. (afterwards Sir) John Soane.

Coll. : *Sir John Soane Museum, London.*

28. IN BEDLAM. Oil on canvas, 24½ × 29½ inches.

In Hogarth's time Bedlam was open to the public and it was a fashionable entertainment for ladies and gentlemen of leisure to go and look at and be amused by the inmates.

29. HIS LEVÉE. Oil on canvas, 24½ × 29½ inches.

Some of the principal figures are portraits of well-known contemporary personalities. Among them are : Essex, the dancing-master ; Figg (died 1734), the prize-fighter ; Bridgeman, the landscape gardener ; Dubois, the Irish fencing-master, who was killed in a duel by a Frenchman of the same name in 1734. The identification of the musician as Handel is very doubtful. The title of the music in front of him is '*The Rape of the Sabines*, an Opera by F. H.' The inscription on the cup, held up by a jockey in the right foreground, reads : ' Won at New Market Sept. 10. 17–(?). Silly Tom.'

30. THE ORGY. (HE REVELS.) Oil on canvas, 24½ × 29½ inches.

The scene takes place in Drury Lane, at the ' Rose Tavern,' the name of which appears on the silver dish, which a man is seen carrying in the left background of the picture. The model for this man is stated to have been Leathercoat, a porter at the tavern. The dish was used by the ' posture-woman,' who is undressing in the foreground, to ' whirl herself round, and display other feats of indecent activity ' ; ' Il suffit ' (I transcribe from Rouquet,[1] who is more circumstantial) ' de vous laisser à deviner la destination de la chandelle. Ce grand plat va servir à cette femme comme à une poularde. Il sera mis au milieu de la table ; elle s'y placera sur le dos ; et l'ivresse et l'esprit de débauche feront trouver plaisant un jeu, qui de sang-froid ne le paroît guères.' (Cf. John Nichols and George Steevens, *The Genuine Works of William Hogarth*, 1810, vol. II, pp. 119–120.)

The incident between two women, depicted in the centre of the painting, is mentioned by J. T. Smith in his *Nollekens and his Times* : ' Hogarth, who was a great frequenter of houses supported by libertines, went to Moll King's, in Covent Garden, accompanied by his friend Hayman, who was at all times highly delighted to see that " moral teacher of mankind " sketch from nature. They had not been in the brothel ten minutes before Hogarth took out his book to draw two ladies whose dispute bespoke a warm contest ; and, at last, one of them, who had taken a mouthful of wine or gin, squirted it in the other's face, which so delighted the artist, that he exclaimed, " Frank, mind the b——'s mouth ! " This incident Hogarth has introduced in the third plate of his Rake's Progress.'

THE ELECTION

Figures 31 and 32 are the two first paintings of a series of four, satirising parliamentary elections. ' The Election ' series was painted in 1755 and sold by Hogarth to Garrick. The circumstances of the sale, as told by Mrs. Garrick, are recorded in a letter of G. Garrard, A.R.A., to Sir John Soane : ' Hogarth called upon her husband one day to solicit his subscription to a set of pictures which he could get no single purchaser for, and therefore proposed to make a raffle of them, that they might not be unpurchased, and Garrick rudely promised to call and look at the pictures—which he did in a few days, and liking the work he gave his name to the subscription—but, when he was to leave the house, just as he was pulling the door after him, his heart struck him, and he said to himself, " Good God, what have I been doing, for this amiable

---

[1] Jean André Rouquet (1702-1759), painter and author, published in Paris in 1746 a *Lettre de M. . . . à un de ses amis pour lui expliquer les estampes d'Hogarth.*

man, my companion and friend, is in want of a small sum to compensate his labour, and I have in a manner refused him. I will return to his room and become the purchaser at once and save him from any further disgrace or trouble." He went back and gave Hogarth the full amount he wanted, £200, and I believe my husband never laid out his money to better advantage.' (Cf. *The Portrait of Sir John Soane, R.A.*, edited by Arthur J. Bolton, p. 364.)

The paintings hung in the Garricks' villa at Hampton and were purchased at Mrs. Garrick's sale in 1823 for 1650 guineas by Sir John Soane.

Coll. : *Sir John Soane Museum, London.*

31. AN ELECTION ENTERTAINMENT. Oil on canvas, 39¾×51 inches.

On one banner is the inscription : ' Marry and multiply in spite of the Devil ' ; on another : ' Give us our eleven days '—a reference to the change of the calendar from the Old Style to the New, which was decreed in 1752 and caused serious rioting, as many people of the lower classes believed that their lives were being shortened by eleven days.

According to George Steevens, Hogarth assured him that there was only one actual portrait in this painting—' the Irish gentleman (Sir John Parnell, nephew to the poet, and remarkable for a very fat nose), who is diverting the company by a face drawn with a burnt cork upon the back of his hand, while he is supposed to be singing *An Old Woman clothed in Grey.*'

Exhibited at the ' Society of Arts ' in Spring Gardens in 1761.

Engraved by Hogarth, and published in 1755.

32. CANVASSING FOR VOTES. Oil on canvas, 39¾×51 inches.

Over the signboard of the ' Royal Oak ' tavern is affixed an election poster in two compartments, one depicting secret service money being rushed out of the Treasury, and the other Punch ladling out gold coins from a barrow. Underneath is the inscription : ' Punch Candidate for Guzzledown.'

Engraved by C. Grigniou, and published in 1757.

33. THE STAYMAKER. Oil on canvas, 28×36 inches.

A sketch of uncertain date.

Etched by Joseph Haynes in 1782.

Former collections : S. Ireland ; W. B. Tiffin, of the Strand ; Forman ; Fairfax Murray ; Agnew.

Coll. : *Sir Edmund Davis, Chilham Castle, Kent.*

34, 35. BEFORE and AFTER. Companion pieces, oil on canvas, 15⅝×13⅜ inches.

Engraved by Hogarth, and published in 1736.

In Hogarth's memorandum dated 1st January 1731, of ' pictures that then remained unfinished, and the half-payment for which had been received,' are mentioned ' Two little pictures, called Before and After, for Mr. Thomson, Dec. 7, 1730.' These belonged afterwards to Lord Bessborough, and in 1833 to H. R. Willett (cf. Austin Dobson, *William Hogarth*, 1907, p. 198). A. Dobson also mentions another version of the two pictures which ' belonged in 1842 to Mr. H. R. Willett ; afterwards to Mr. Locker Lampson ; now the property of the Duke of Hamilton (17½×12½ inches).' A replica of ' Before ' is in the Royal Collection.

The present paintings were formerly in the possession of the Leicester Galleries, London.

Coll. : *Thorsten Laurin, Esq., Stockholm.*

36, 37. BEER STREET and GIN LANE. Companion pieces, red-chalk drawings.

The original drawings for the prints which were engraved by Hogarth, and published in 1751. Hogarth gives the following account of them : ' When these two Prints were designed and engraved, the dreadful consequences of gin-drinking appeared in every street. In *Gin-Lane*, every circumstance of its horrid effects is brought to view *in terrorem*. Idleness, poverty, misery, and distress, which drives even to madness and death, are the only objects that are to be seen ; and not a house in tolerable condition, but the Pawnbroker's and Gin-shop. *Beer-Street*, its companion, was given as a contrast ; where that invigorating liquor is recommended, in order to drive the other out of vogue. Here all is joyous, and thriving industry and jollity go hand in hand. In this happy place the Pawnbroker's is the only house going to ruin ; and even the small quantity of porter that he can procure is taken in at the wicket, for fear of further distress.' (Cf. John Ireland, *Hogarth Illustrated*, vol. III.)

The drawings vary considerably in detail from the prints.

Former collections : Joly ; Fairfax Murray.

We have been unable to ascertain the present ownership of the drawings.

38. A DANCE AT THE WANSTEAD ASSEMBLY. Oil on canvas, $26\frac{1}{2} \times 35$ inches.

Wanstead House, Essex, which was demolished in the earlier part of the nineteenth century, was built by Earl Tylney about 1715. The figures in the picture are said to represent the Earl, his wife, children and tenants.

The present painting is a sketch, probably executed in 1728–29. It has been identified by Austin Dobson (cf. his *William Hogarth*, 1907) as 'The Country Dance,' illustrated in Hogarth's *Analysis of Beauty*, published in 1753. In the artist's list of 1st January 1731, enumerating the 'pictures that then remained unfinished, and the half-payment for which had been received,' is mentioned 'an Assembly of twenty-five figures, for Lord Castlemain, August 28, 1729.' ' The Wanstead Assembly ' figured at the exhibition of Hogarth's works held at the British Gallery in 1814 ; it is stated in the catalogue as being ' in the possession of W. Long Wellesley, Esq.' The present sketch was exhibited in 1875 by W. Carpenter, of Forest Hill, and was bequeathed by him in 1899 to the South London Art Gallery. In the *Commemorative Catalogue of the Exhibition of British Art*, 1934, where it was exhibited as *A Masked Ball at Wanstead Assembly* (no masks appear in the picture), its previous owners are given as ' S. Ireland, Gt. Vernon, 1801 ; W. B. Tiffin of the Strand in 1833 ; W. Carpenter in 1875.'

Coll. : *South London Art Gallery, Camberwell.*

HAMILTON, GAWEN, Attributed to (1697–1737)

39. LONDON STREET SCENE. Oil on canvas, $22\frac{1}{2} \times 30$ inches.

Coll. : *Dr. Douglas McAlpine, London.*

HAYMAN, FRANCIS (1708–1776)

40. THE MERRYMAKERS. Oil on canvas, 31×48 inches.

Engraved as ' The Wapping Landlady ' by Benoist in 1743.

Formerly the property of Sir Oswald Mosley.

Coll. : *Mrs. F. S. Collins, London.*

PETERS, THE REV. MATTHEW WILLIAM, R.A. (1742–1814)

41. CHILDREN. Oil on canvas, $25\frac{1}{4} \times 30\frac{3}{4}$ inches.

Diploma work deposited at the Royal Academy by the artist on his election as an Academician in 1777. Engraved by J. B. Michel in 1786.

Coll. : *Diploma Gallery, Royal Academy of Arts, London.*

42. LYDIA. Oil on canvas, $24\frac{1}{2} \times 29\frac{1}{2}$ inches.

There are several versions of this picture, one of identical size being in the collection of the Marquess of Lansdowne. One of these was originally painted for Earl Grosvenor and exhibited at the Royal Academy in 1777 with the title ' A Woman in Bed.' It then roused the indignation of the critic of the *Morning Chronicle*, who wrote that ' in its present situation it serves to prevent the pictures round it from being so much seen and admired as their merits demand, for every man who has either his wife or his daughter with him must for decency's sake hurry them away from that corner of the room.' (Cf. Whitley, *Artists and their Friends, 1700–1799*, 1928, vol. I, p. 349.)

Engraved by W. Dickinson in 1776.

Former collections : Agnew ; Barnett Lewis.

Coll. : *The Earl of Granard, Castle Forbes, Co. Longford.*

LAROON, JOHN MARCELLUS (1679–1772)

43. INTERIOR WITH FIGURES. Oil on canvas, 17×15 inches.

Sometimes referred to as ' Tavern Scene.'
Formerly in the collection of Mr. Julian Lousada, who presented the painting to the nation in 1928 through the National Art Collections Fund.
Coll. : *The Tate Gallery, Millbank, London.*

JOHNSON, THOMAS (Active 1651–1685)

44. THE BATHS AT BATH. Indian ink, wash and pen drawing, 13¼×18⅝ inches.

Inscribed on the top part of the drawing is a key indicating the particular parts of the baths. The large bath on the right was called ' the King's Bath,' the smaller one on the left ' the Queen's.' The inscription next to the key reads as follows :

> BLADUD, SON TO LUDHUDEBRAS,
> THE EIGHT KING OF THE BRITAINS,
> FROM BRUTE, A GREAT PHILOSOPHER,
> AND MATHEMATITIAN : BRED AT ATHENS,
> AND RECORDED THE FIRST DISCOVERER,
> AND FOUNDER OF THESE BATHS, EIGHT
> HUNDRED SIXTY AND THREE YEARES
> BEFORE CHRIST, THAT IS TWO THOUSAND
> FIVE HUNDRED THIRTY FIVE YEARS
> SINCE
> ANNO DOMINI 1672

The balusters of the parapet on top of the house above the Queen's Bath compose the dedication :

> ANNAE REGINAE SACRUM 1618

Signed and dated : *T. Johnson Delineat*, 1675.
Purchased in 1881.
Coll. : *The British Museum, London.*

BARLOW, FRANCIS (*c.* 1626–1702)

45. A FARMYARD WITH FIGURES AND LANDSCAPE BACKGROUND. Indian ink drawing, 7⅜×9⅝ inches.
Coll. : *Victoria and Albert Museum, London.*

MONAMY, PETER (*c.* 1670–1749)

46. THE OLD EAST INDIA WHARF AT LONDON BRIDGE. Oil on canvas, 63×54 inches.
Coll. : *Victoria and Albert Museum, London.*

VAN AKEN, JOSEF, Attributed to (1709–1749)

47. A VILLAGE SCHOOL. Oil on canvas, 18×23 inches.
Coll. : *Sir Edward Marsh, London.*

HODGES, WILLIAM, R.A. (1744–1797)

48. INTERIOR WITH FIGURES. Oil on canvas, 24×27 inches.

This painting was included in a sale at Sotheby's on 30th March 1927. We have been unable to ascertain the present ownership of the picture.

WRIGHT, JOSEPH, A.R.A. (WRIGHT OF DERBY) (1734–1797)

49. THE IRON FORGE. Oil on canvas, 56¾×60⅝ inches.
Exhibited at the Society of Artists in 1772.
Engraved by Richard Earlom in 1773.
Coll. : *Lord Mount Temple, Broadlands.*

50. THE OLD MAN AND DEATH. Oil on canvas, 25×30 inches.

There exists a larger (40×50 inches) version of this picture. A painting with this title was exhibited by Wright at the Society of Artists in 1774.

Coll. : *Mrs. Kilburn Milroy Bright, Barton Court, Colwall, Malvern.*

51. THE ORRERY. Oil on canvas, 58×80 inches.

The figures are portraits and represent : Denby, organist at All Saints', Derby, as the philosopher in the centre ; Mrs. Sale seated on extreme left ; Peter Perez Burdett, the engraver, above her, taking notes ; Lawrence Rowland Shirley (1757-1773), son of Robert, sixth Earl Ferrers—the boy seated next to Burdett ; Joseph Wright on extreme right. The others are said to be young Cantrell, A. Winterman and G. Snowden.

Painted for the sixth Earl Ferrers in 1766 and exhibited in the same year at the Society of Artists with the title ' A Philosopher giving that Lecture on the Orrery, in which a lamp is put in the place of the Sun.'

Engraved in mezzotint by William Pether in 1768, and by Val. Green.

Formerly the property of John Wright, of Osmanton Manor, from whom the picture was purchased for the Gallery in 1884.

Coll. : *Corporation Art Gallery, Derby.*

MORLAND, GEORGE (1763-1804)

52. THE FRUITS OF EARLY INDUSTRY AND ECONOMY. Oil on canvas, 30×24½ inches.

Companion piece to ' The Effects of Youthful Extravagance.' Both pictures were engraved by W. Ward in 1789. They were included in a sale at Christie's in 1809 as the property of ' a publisher ' (J. Simpson ?) and fetched together 85 guineas.

Coll. : *McFadden Collection, Philadelphia.*

53. THE COTTAGE DOOR. Oil on panel, 13½×17½ inches.

Formerly called ' The Contented Waterman ' and also referred to as ' My Poll and my partner Joe.'

Signed and dated : *G. Morland,* 1790.

Engraved by W. Ward in 1790 and 1806, and by R. Clamp in 1797.

Former collections : George Tierney ; Thomas Holloway.

Coll. : *Royal Holloway College, Englefield Green, London.*

54. A VISIT TO THE BOARDING SCHOOL. Oil on canvas, 23⅝×28¾ inches.

Signed : *G. Morland.*

Engraved by W. Ward in 1789 as a companion piece to ' A Visit to the Child at Nurse ' (1788).

Purchased by Sir Richard Wallace in 1873 from H. Durlacher for £500.

Coll. : *The Wallace Collection, London.*

COLLETT, JOHN (1725-1780)

55. NINEPINS. Oil on canvas 13⅝×10⅝ inches.

The inscription on the keystone of the arch reads : ' Miss Tipapin going for all nine.' Collett did a set of six paintings entitled ' Ladies' Recreations,' of which this picture is number five.

Coll. : *Viscount Bearsted, M.C., Upton House, Banbury.*

SMITH, JOHN RAPHAEL (1752-1812)

56. A PROMENADE AT CARLISLE HOUSE, SOHO SQUARE. Crayon drawing, coloured, oval, 12$\frac{5}{16}$×15$\frac{5}{16}$ inches.

According to an old identification the figures from left to right are : Mrs. Moss, two unknown gentlemen, Charlotte Somerville, Mary Townley, Maria Welldon, Harriet Montague, Dr. Johnson(?), Lucy Haswell and J. R. Smith.

Carlisle House stood on the east side of Soho Square, at the corner of Sutton Street. It was pulled down at the end of the eighteenth century. The site of its former ballroom is now occupied by St. Patrick's Roman Catholic Church. In 1760 Carlisle House was taken over from the Earls of Carlisle by the notorious Theresa Cornelys (1723-1797), who, according to Walpole, ' made her house a fairy palace for balls, concerts and masquerades ' (letter to Sir Horace Mann, 22nd February 1771), and organised there the fashionable assemblies of ' The Circle of Carlisle House.' In 1778 Mrs. Cornelys failed, but the Carlisle House entertainments were continued for some time under another management.

Engraved by J. R. Smith, and published in 1781.
Coll. : *Victoria and Albert Museum, London.*

WHEATLEY, FRANCIS, R.A. (1747-1801)

57. A Holiday Resort with Gipsies. Water-colour, 17½×25½ inches.

A water-colour identical in composition except for the two figures and the tree in the foreground is in the collection of Count Matsukata, Japan.

Signed and dated : *F. Wheatley, 1794.*
Coll. : *Lord Brocket, Brocket Hall, Welwyn.*

The Life of a Country Girl

Figures 58, 59, 60 and 61 are companion pieces which form a set entitled ' The Life of a Country Girl.' The individual titles of the paintings are :

58. Maidenhood.

59. Courtship.

60. Marriage.

61. Married Life.

Oil on canvas, 31½×26½ inches.
Exhibited at the Royal Academy in 1792 with the titles : ' The Maternal Blessing,' ' The Offer of Marriage,' ' The Wedding Morning,' and ' The happy Fireside.'
Formerly in the collection of Sir Randolf L. Baker, Bt.
Coll. : *Viscount Bearsted, Upton House, Banbury.*

WILLIAMS, WILLIAM

(Practised in London in the later half of the eighteenth century, was awarded a premium by the Society of Arts in 1758, and was an occasional exhibitor at the Royal Academy between 1770 and 1792.)

62. Courtship.

63. Marriage.

Companion pieces, oil on canvas, 31⅜×16⅜ inches.
Signed and dated : *W. Williams, 1797.*
Former collections : Agnew (sale at Christie's in 1923) ; The Knoedler Galleries.
We have been unable to ascertain the present ownership of these paintings.

WALTON, HENRY (1764-1813)

64. The Cherry Seller. Oil on canvas, 30×25 inches.

Also known as ' The Fruit Barrow.'
Engraved by J. R. Smith.
Coll. : *Captain Osbert Sitwell, Renishaw Hall, Derbyshire.*

65. A pretty Maid buying a Love song. Oil on canvas, 42×34 inches.
Exhibited at the Royal Academy in 1778.
Engraved by F. Bartolozzi and I. Walker in 1785.
Coll. : *Lord Mildmay of Flete, London.*

MALTON, JAMES (*c.* 1766–1803)

66. CAPEL STREET, DUBLIN. Water-colour, 23⅛×31 inches.

In the distance is the Royal Exchange.
Signed and dated 1800.
Coll. : *Victoria and Albert Museum, London.*

REPTON, HUMPHREY (1752–1818)

67. THE PUMP ROOM AT BATH. Water-colour, 17¼×23¾ inches.

Inscribed on the top : ' The Pump Room, Bath ' and ' Qui capit, ille facit.' The verse at
the bottom of the drawing runs as follows :

' Hither the Sick, the Gay, the Old, the Young,
Impell'd by Hope of Change, successive throng ;
Here the light Widow, ogling every Beau,
Hopes to forget, and get a Husband too ;
Here Fops get Fortunes, Cit's get rid of Cares,
And doating Husbands fancy they get Heirs.'

The figures are various characters of the day, but the old key to their names has been lost.
One of the very few examples of Repton's drawings not connected with garden scenery.
Humphrey Repton was the great landscape gardener, whose most famous creation is Longleat
in Wiltshire.
Signed and dated : *H. Repton,* 1784.
Exhibited at the Royal Academy in 1787.
Coll. : *Guy Repton, Esq., London.*

COLLINGS, SAMUEL

(Exhibited at the Royal Academy from 1784 to 1789)

68. FROST ON THE THAMES, SKETCHED ON THE SPOT. Oil.

Painted during the winter 1788–89, which was the last time but one that the Thames was
frozen over in London. The figure on the extreme left is believed to be the portrait of the artist.
Exhibited at the Royal Academy in 1789.
Coll. : *Dr. Louis C. Parkes.*

BRETHERTON, CHARLES (*c.* 1760–1783)

69. A TRIP TO SCARBOROUGH. Water-colour, 9½×19 inches.

Painted about 1780. The Sketch for a print published in 1783.
Coll. : *The Marquess of Lansdowne, Bowood, Calne, Wiltshire.*

DIGHTON, ROBERT (1752–1814)

70. THE WESTMINSTER ELECTION, 1788. Pen and Water-colour, 15½×19 inches.

The scene takes place at Covent Garden. In the foreground stands Lord John Townshend
(1757–1833), who in this election was victorious over Admiral Lord Hood (1724–1816). Next
to him are Georgiana Duchess of Devonshire (1757–1806), her sister, Lady Duncannon, and
John Wilkes (1727–1797), who has his pocket picked by a boy. Above him a man is holding
up Fox's election mascot. In the carriage is the Prince of Wales with a lady.
Dighton made drawings of the Westminster Elections of 1784, 1788 and 1796. The 1784
drawing, which was exhibited at the Royal Academy in 1785, is now lost. The 1796 drawing is
in the Royal collection.
Signed : *Dighton Del.*
Coll. : *Ralph Edwards, Esq., London.*

71. MEN OF WAR BOUND FOR THE PORT OF PLEASURE. Monochrome drawing tinted with water-colour, $12\frac{5}{8} \times 9\frac{7}{8}$ inches.

The scene represents a wharf at Gravesend, which was the starting place of the Chatham Tide Coach, seen in the background.
Signed : *R. Dighton del.*
Purchased by the Museum in 1875.
Coll. : *The British Museum, London.*

STUBBS, GEORGE, A.R.A. (1724–1806)

72. THE REAPERS.

73. THE HAYMAKERS : LATE AFTERNOON.

Companion pieces, oil on panel, 36×54 inches.
Signed and dated 1783.
Exhibited at the Royal Academy in 1786.
Engraved by Stubbs, and published in 1791.
Formerly in the collection of Sir Walter Gilbey.
Coll. : *Viscount Bearstead, Upton House, Banbury.*

LEWIS, GEORGE ROBERT (1782–1871)

74. VIEW IN HEREFORDSHIRE : HARVEST. Oil on canvas, $16\frac{3}{8} \times 23\frac{1}{2}$ inches.

Painted about 1817. Inscribed on the back : *Hereford, Dynedor and Malvern Hills from Haywood Lodge. Geo. Lewis, 9, Southampton Row, New Road, Paddington.*
Presented to the Gallery by the Rev. Stopford Brooke in 1914.
Coll. : *The Tate Gallery, Millbank, London.*

GAINSBOROUGH, THOMAS, R.A. (1727–1788)

75. THE HARVEST WAGGON. Oil on canvas, $47\frac{1}{4} \times 57$ inches.

The landscape represents a view at Shockerwick, near Bath. The artist's daughters, Mary and Margaret, posed for the girl getting into the waggon and the girl seated in it, looking upward. The grey horse belonged to the carrier Wiltshire, who used to convey the artist's pictures from Bath to the exhibitions in London. When Gainsborough left Bath in 1774 Wiltshire gave him the horse in exchange for ' The Harvest Waggon.' There is an earlier version of the same subject in the collection of Sir Lionel Phillips.
Exhibited at the Royal Academy in 1771.
Former Collections : Mr. Wiltshire ; sold at Christie's in 1867 ; Davies ; Lord Tweedmouth. Acquired by the present owner in 1904.
Coll. : *Lord Swaythling, Townhill Park.*

BIGG, WILLIAM REDMORE, R.A. (1755–1828)

76. TREPANNING A RECRUIT. Oil on canvas, 34×43 inches.

The scene depicts army recruiting during the Napoleonic Wars and is set outside a country inn which bears the sign of the swan.
Presented to the Gallery by George Knight, Esq.
Coll. : *The Russell-Cotes Art Gallery and Museum, Bournemouth.*

WARD, JAMES, R.A. (1769–1859)

77. THE WOUNDED SOLDIER. Oil on canvas, $19\frac{5}{8} \times 25\frac{5}{8}$ inches.

A companion piece to this picture, entitled ' The Recruit,' is in the same collection.
Engraved in mezzotint by J. R. Smith and published in 1803.
Coll. : *J. J. Tufnell, Esq., Chelmsford.*

BURNEY, EDWARD FRANCIS (1760–1848)

78. DRAWING TAUGHT IN ALL ITS BRANCHES. Drawing, $25\frac{1}{2} \times 14\frac{1}{2}$ inches.

Sold at Christie's in 1925 to Major Thomas Sutton, Lewes.
We have been unable to ascertain the present ownership of the drawing.

79. AN ELEGANT ESTABLISHMENT FOR YOUNG LADIES. Water-colour, $19\frac{3}{8} \times 28\frac{1}{2}$ inches.

Purchased at Col. Henry Burney's sale in 1930 by Messrs. Thomas Agnew and Sons, and presented by them to the Museum.
Coll. : *Victoria and Albert Museum, London.*

HEIGHWAY, RICHARD (Attributed to)

(Exhibited at the Royal Academy between 1787 and 1793)

80. THE POULTRY SELLER. Oil on canvas, $26 \times 21\frac{1}{2}$ inches.
Coll. : *Victoria and Albert Museum, London.*

MACLISE, DANIEL, R.A. (1811–1870)

81. GIRL AT THE WATERFALL AT ST. NECTAN'S OR NIGHTON'S KIEVE, NEAR TINTAGEL, CORNWALL. Oil on canvas, $35\frac{1}{2} \times 27\frac{3}{4}$ inches.

The model for the figure was Miss Georgina Hogarth, sister-in-law of Charles Dickens.
Signed and dated : *D. Maclise, R.A.,* 1842.
The picture was bought from the artist in 1843 by Charles Dickens, and purchased at the latter's sale in 1870 by John Foster, who bequeathed it to the Museum.
Coll. : *Victoria and Albert Museum, London.*

DE LOUTHERBOURG, PHILIP JACOB, R.A. (1740–1812)

82. A MIDSUMMER'S AFTERNOON WITH A METHODIST PREACHER. Oil on canvas, 37×49 inches.

A note in the catalogue of the Burlington Fine Arts Club Winter Exhibition, 1927–28, where the picture was exhibited, states that ' when purchased some years ago, the preacher had been painted over with a " polichinello." On its removal the features of the preacher were approximated to those of Wesley. Scenes such as these were common in 1765–75, and were parodied in a much-read novel, *The Spiritual Quixote,* by Richard Graves, 1772, an episode from which this picture may represent.' Though it has formerly been called 'Wesley preaching on a Green,' there is no foundation to the assumption that the preacher is Wesley.
The picture was first exhibited as ' Methodist Preacher ' at the Royal Academy in 1777, when the following comment on it appeared in the *Public Advertiser* : ' It is but doing common justice to this ingenious foreigner to assert that he has carried the diversity of English character in this piece to as great a height as it was ever carried, even by the great Hogarth himself in the first of his productions ; nay, further, as he expresses all his humour in a correcter style of proportion.'
There is another version of the same subject in a private collection in America.
Signed and dated : *P. J. De Loutherbourg,* 1777.
Former collections : Col. W. F. Tipping ; H. Avray Tipping ; Colnaghi.
Coll. : *The National Gallery of Canada, Ottawa.*

HAYDON, BENJAMIN ROBERT (1786–1846)

83. PUNCH, OR MAY DAY. Oil on canvas, $58\frac{1}{2} \times 72$ inches.

The scene takes place in front of Marylebone Church. Originally entitled ' Life in London.'
On 15th April 1829 Haydon wrote in his *Journals* :
' Yesterday, when I rubbed in " Punch," my thoughts crowded with delight. My children's noise hurt my brain. At such moments no silence is great enough, but I am never let alone. Good God ! What I should have produced had I been let loose in a great place, and saved from disturbing embarrassment.'
The picture was completed by November 1829 and exhibited at a gallery in Bond Street

early in the following year. On 6th March 1830 it was sent to Windsor to be inspected by King George IV, and on 8th March appears the following entry in the artist's *Journals* :

'The " Punch " came back (from Windsor) to-day. I called on Sequier in the morning, but I saw by the girl's face at the door the King had not bought the picture. The King thought there was too much " Punch." He admired the apple-girl excessively, but thought the capering chimney-sweeper too much like an opera dancer.'

Formerly the property of Dr. George Darling, who bequeathed the painting to the Gallery in 1862.

Coll. : *The Tate Gallery, Millbank, London.*

FÜSSLI, JOHANN HEINRICH, KNOWN AS FUSELI, HENRY, R.A. (1741–1825)

84. THE NIGHTMARE. Oil on canvas, 30×25 inches.

Painted about 1782 and exhibited in that year at the Royal Academy, where it met with the disapproval of Walpole, who pronounced it to be ' shocking.'

The story is told that Fuseli conceived ' The Nightmare ' during an attack of indigestion caused by eating raw pork. The truth of this story is disbelieved by W. T. Whitley, who sees its origin in a humorous paragraph on Fuseli which appeared in the *Public Advertiser* in 1790, and where reference is made to ' a circumstance not generally known, but which is equally interesting to the Poet, the Naturalist, and the Physician. It is a fact that this creative fancy springs solely from an *animal process*, and is brought about after regular intervals by Mr. Fuseli's *eating raw pork for supper*. The fact of indigestion producing a strong effect on the imagination is fully ascertained. The monstrous forms which the latter brings in consequence are immediately sketched, and if necessary embodied on the canvas. This account, however it may border on the ludicrous, our readers may rely on as strictly founded on truth.' (Cf. W. T. Whitley, *Art in England*, 1821–1837, p. 85.)

Haydon made the following entry in his *Journals* in March 1825 : ' Fuseli is dead. . . . Notwithstanding the apathy of the public latterly towards his works, Fuseli had had his day. His " Nightmare " was decidedly popular all over Europe. Fuseli was paid £30 for the picture, and the engraver cleared £600 by the print.'

' The Nightmare ' was engraved and published by J. R. Smith.

A replica of the painting is in the collection of the Earl of Harrowby, Stafford. Fuseli also produced several other variations of the subject, which are of later date.

Coll. : *Professor Paul Ganz, Basle.*

LAWRENCE, SIR THOMAS, P.R.A. (1769–1830)

85. THE DEMOLITION OF THE DOMINICAN CHAPEL AT GENOA. Oil on canvas, 23×16 inches.

Signed, dated and inscribed across the bottom of the picture : *Thomas Lawrence, demolition of Dominican Friars Abbey in Genoa*, 1819.

Lawrence visited Genoa during his journey abroad in 1818–1819.

Another view of the same town, painted at the same time and representing the ' Porta Soprana ' is in the collection of M. de Pasquali, Genoa.

Formerly in the possession of M. Egisto de Masi, Genoa.

Coll. : *Duc de Trévise, Paris.*

PALMER, SAMUEL (1805–1881)

86. SHEEP-SHEARING. Oil on panel, 19¾×27½ inches.

An early work, painted in the Shoreham period (1826–1833).

Coll. : *Henry Reitlinger, Esq., London.*

COTMAN, JOHN SELL (1782–1842)

87. THE MARKET PLACE, NORWICH. Pencil drawing tinted with water-colour, 14×21¼ inches.

The drawing was done from the house of a silversmith called Cooper, which stood at the north-east corner of the Square, looking out on the Church of St. Peter Mancroft. It was exhibited at Norwich in 1807 as ' A coloured sketch of the Market Place, Norwich, taken from

Mr. Cooper's.' It used to belong to the Quaker poet and friend of Charles Lamb—Bernard Barton, who wrote a poem ' On a Drawing of Norwich Market Place, by Cotman, taken in 1807.' (Cf. Sydney D. Kitson, *The Life of John Sell Cotman*, 1937, p. 109.)

Signed and dated : *J. S. Cotman*, 1807.

Former Collections : Bernard Barton ; Mrs. Edward Fitzgerald ; Capt. F. R. Barton.

Coll. : *Mrs. Esmond Morse, Claughton Hall, Hornby.*

TURNER, JOSEPH MALLORD WILLIAM, R.A. (1775–1851)

88. THE HOE, PLYMOUTH. Water-colour, 11 × 16¼ inches.

Engraved in *Picturesque Views in England and Wales*, 1832.

Bequeathed to the Museum by John Jones.

Coll. : *Victoria and Albert Museum, London.*

FERNELEY, JOHN (1781–1860)

89. THE HORSE FAIR, MELTON MOWBRAY. Oil on canvas, 25 × 33 inches.

Signed and dated : *J. Ferneley, June 14th* 1835.

Former collections : Marshall Field, Esq. ; the Knoedler Galleries.

Coll. : *Private collection, America.*

HAVELL, WILLIAM (1782–1857)

90. THE OLD HAMPTON FERRY AND RACECOURSE. Oil on canvas, 21½ × 51½ inches.

According to an inscription on the frame the picture was painted in 1821.

Coll. : *The Redfern Gallery, London.*

ETTY, WILLIAM, R.A. (1787–1849)

91. A CONVERSATION. Oil, 16 × 11½ inches.

Coll. : *Hon. Mr. Justice F. F. Madan, London.*

WEBSTER, THOMAS, R.A. (1800–1886)

92. THE RETURN FROM THE FAIR. Oil on panel, 22 × 30 inches.

A companion piece to ' Going to the Fair ' in the same collection. Both pictures were painted for a Mr. Flood.

Signed and dated : *T. Webster*, 1837.

Exhibited at the British Institution in 1838.

Presented to the Museum by John Sheepshanks in 1857.

Coll. : *Victoria and Albert Museum, London.*

OPIE, JOHN, R.A. (1761–1807)

93. THE SCHOOLMISTRESS. Oil on canvas, 39¼ × 49¼ inches.

Exhibited at the Royal Academy in 1784 as ' The School.' Walpole's comment on it was : ' Great nature, the best of his works yet.'

Another version of this picture was exhibited by the Earl of Stamford and Warrington at the Art Treasure Exhibition in Manchester in 1857.

Former collections : G. Watson Taylor ; Chantry ; Russell ; Agnew ; Lord Overstone ; Lord Wantage.

Coll. : *A. T. Loyd, Esq., Lockinge House, Wanstead.*

MULREADY, WILLIAM, R.A. (1786–1863)

94. THE FIGHT INTERRUPTED. Oil on panel, 28½ × 37 inches.

Painted for Lord Whitworth, Viceroy of Ireland, in 1815.

Signed : *W. Mul*, and dated 1816—the year when the picture was exhibited at the Royal Academy.

After Lord Whitworth's death it passed into the possession of the Earl de la Warr and was later purchased from him by John Sheepshanks, who presented it to the Museum in 1857.

Coll. : *Victoria and Albert Museum, London.*

95. THE CONVALESCENT FROM WATERLOO. Oil on panel, 24×30½ inches.

Painted in 1822, and exhibited at the Royal Academy in the same year.
Bequeathed to the Museum by Mr. John Jones.
Coll. : *Victoria and Albert Museum, London.*

CRUIKSHANK, GEORGE (1792–1878)

96. GRIMALDI SHAVED BY A GIRL.

Joseph Grimaldi, the famous clown, was born in 1779 and died in 1837.
Painted in 1838—the same year when Cruikshank illustrated the *Memoirs of Joseph Grimaldi*, edited by ' Boz.'
We have been unable to trace the original painting or to find any further information about it. It is presumably in the U.S.A.

97. THE DISTURBER DETECTED. Oil on panel, 16½×20¾ inches.

Painted in 1850 and purchased by the Prince Consort.
Coll. : *His Majesty the King, Windsor Castle.*

98. THE GHOST. Wash, sepia, touched with red and heightened with white on blue-grey paper, 5×4⅝ inches.

Signed : *G. Cruikshank.*
Sold in the Newman Sale at the American Art Association Anderson Galleries Inc., New York, on 2nd February 1927.

99. THE WORSHIP OF BACCHUS, OR THE DRINKING CUSTOMS OF SOCIETY. Oil on canvas, 92×159 inches.

Painted in 1862. Exhibited in 1863 at a small gallery in Wellington Street, Strand, and taken by Royal command to Windsor for Queen Victoria's inspection. It was later exhibited in various provincial towns, and eventually, in 1869, presented to the nation by R. E. Lofft and other friends of the artist.
Thackeray wrote in *The Times* of 15th May 1863 an article where he says about this picture :
' For upwards of half a century, he (Cruikshank) says he has employed pencil and pen against the vice of drunkenness, and in the vain attempt to shut up drinking shops and to establish *moderate drinking as a universal rule* ; but for seventeen years he has discovered that teetotalism or the total abstaining from all intoxicating liquors, was the only real remedy for the entire abolition of intemperance. His thoughts working in this direction, one day this subject of " The Worship of Bacchus " flashed across his mind, and hence the origin of a work of art measuring 13 ft. 4 in. by 7 ft. 8 in., which has occupied the author no less than a year and a half.
' This sermon has the advantage over others, that you can take a chapter at a time, as it were, and return and resume the good homilist's discourse at your leisure. What is your calling in life ? In some part of this vast tableau you will find it is *de te fabula*. In this compartment the soldiers are drinking " Healths to the young Christian." Here are the publicans, filthily intoxicated with their own horrible liquors ; yonder is a masquerade supper, " where drunken masquerade fiends drag down columbines to drunkenness and ruin." Near them are " the public singers chanting forth the praises of the ' God of Wine.' " " Is it not marvellous to think," says Mr. Cruikshank in a little pamphlet containing a speech by him which is quite as original as the picture on which it comments, " is it not marvellous what highly talented poetry and what harmonious musical compositions have been produced, from time to time, in praise of this imaginative, slippery, deceitful, dangerous myth ? "
' " This myth " the spectator may follow all through this most wonderful and labyrinthine picture. In the nursery the doctor is handing a pot of beer to mamma ; the nurse is drinking beer ; the little boy is crying for beer ; and the papa is drawing a cork, so that " he and the doctor may have a drop." Here you have a group of women, victims of intemperance, " tearing, biting, and mutilating one another." Yonder are two of the police carrying away a *drunken policeman*. Does not the mind reel and stagger at the idea of this cumulated horror ? And what is the wine which yonder clergyman holds in his hand but the same kind of stuff which has made the mother in the christening scene above " so tipsy that she has let her child fall out of her lap, while her idiotic husband points to his helpless wife, and exclaims, " Ha, ha ; she's dr-unk ! " '

In the pamphlet on the ' Worship of Bacchus ' referred to by Thackeray, Cruikshank makes the statement that he has ' not the vanity to call it a *picture*, it being the mapping out of certain ideas for an especial purpose, and I painted it with a view that a lecturer might use it as so many diagrams, so that the mind might be operated upon, through the *ear* as well as the *eye*, at the same time.'

In an engraving of the picture published in 1864 the outlines of all the figures were etched by Cruikshank himself and the rest finished by Charles Mottram. (Cf. Blanchard Jerrold, *The Life of George Cruikshank*, 1882.)

The original water-colour sketch for the painting, inscribed : ' Designed and drawn by George Cruikshank, Teetotaler, 1860,' was presented by the artist's widow to the Victoria and Albert Museum (now at the Bethnal Green Museum).

Coll. : *The National Gallery, London.*

DADD, RICHARD (1817–1887)

100. THE FAIRY TELLER'S MASTER-STROKE. Oil on canvas.

Signed, inscribed and dated on the back : *The Fairy Teller's Master-Stroke. Painted for G. H. Haydon, Esq., by Rd. Dadd, quasi—1855–64.*

Former collections : Alfred Morrison ; Lady Gatty.

Coll. : *Siegfried Sassoon, Esq., Heytesbury House, Wiltshire.*

101. IN A CURIOSITY SHOP. Water-colour, $10\frac{1}{8} \times 13\frac{7}{8}$ inches.

Inscribed : *Sketch of A Curiosity Shop, by Richard Dadd, Bethlehem Hospital, London. June 22nd, 1854.*

Dadd became an inmate of Bethlehem Hospital in 1843.

Purchased in 1906.

Coll. : *The British Museum, London.*

WILKIE, SIR DAVID, R.A. (1785–1841)

102. THE FIRST EARRING. Oil on panel, $29 \times 23\frac{1}{2}$ inches.

Signed and dated : *David Wilkie f. 1835.*

Exhibited at the Royal Academy in 1835. Another picture with the same title was exhibited at the Royal Academy in 1836.

Presented to the National Gallery in 1847 by Robert Vernon.

Coll. : *The Tate Gallery, Millbank, London.*

103. READING THE WILL. Oil.

Sketch for the painting which was commissioned by the King of Bavaria and hung after his death in the New Pinacothek, Munich.

Coll. : *The Marquess of Normanton, Somerley, Ringwood, Hampshire.*

104. THE VILLAGE SCHOOL AT PITLESSIE, FIFE. Oil on panel, $40\frac{1}{2} \times 64\frac{1}{2}$ inches.

Coll. : *Major Philip Fleming, London.*

105. NEWSMONGERS. Oil on panel, $16 \times 13\frac{1}{2}$ inches.

Painted for General Phipps.

Exhibited at the Royal Academy in 1812.

Presented to the National Gallery in 1847 by Robert Vernon.

Coll. : *The Tate Gallery, Millbank, London.*

BONINGTON, RICHARD PARKES (1802–1828)

106. THE USE OF TEARS. Oil, $15\frac{1}{4} \times 12\frac{1}{2}$ inches.

Sometimes also called ' The Visit ' and ' The Sick Daughter.'

The picture has been engraved three times : by C. Rolls, S. W. Reynolds (1829) and J. Doney. The engravings differ in details.

Former collections : M. van Praet, Brussels ; Boussod Valadon et Cie, Paris ; Josiah Bradlee, Boston, who bequeathed the picture to the Museum in 1903.

Coll. : *Museum of Fine Arts, Boston, Mass.*

KIDD, WILLIAM (1796–1863)

107. THE TRAVELLING SHOWMAN. Oil on canvas, 34×43 inches.

The scene is laid outside Edinburgh Castle.
Exhibited at the Associated Society of Artists, Edinburgh, in 1810. The previous year, when Kidd exhibited at the same Society 'The Cobbler's Shop,' the notice appeared in the catalogue : ' By W. Kid, aged 13 years, apprentice to J. Howe.'
Coll. : *The Parker Galleries, London.*

BROWNLOW, GEORGE WASHINGTON

(Exhibited at the Royal Academy from 1860 to 1875)

108. CADOGAN PIER, CHELSEA. Oil on canvas, 16¾×20½ inches.

Signed and dated : *W. Brownlow,* 1858.
Exhibited at the British Institution in 1859 with the title : ' Waiting for another fare ; the juvenile conveyance between Cadogan Pier, Chelsea, and Cremorne.'
Coll. : *The Leicester Galleries, London.*

LEWIS, JOHN FREDERICK, R.A. (1805–1876)

109. LILIUM AURATUM. Oil on canvas, 52¾×33¼ inches.

Signed and dated : *J. F. Lewis, R.A.,* 1871.
First exhibited at the Royal Academy in 1872.
Sold by the artist to David Price. Presented to the Gallery by the nephews of G. E. Belliss in 1911.
Coll. : *City of Birmingham Art Gallery.*

110. INDOOR GOSSIP. Oil on panel, 11¾×7¾ inches.

The scene takes place in a harem in Cairo.
Signed and dated : *J. F. Lewis, R.A.,* 1873.
Exhibited at the Royal Academy in 1874.
Coll. : *C. W. Dyson Perrins, Esq., Malvern.*

BROWN, FORD MADOX (1821–1893)

111. THE LAST OF ENGLAND. Oil on wood panel, almost circular, 32¼×29 inches.

Madox Brown first conceived the idea for this picture during a visit to Gravesend in 1851. He started to work on it in 1852, but did not finish it until September 1855. The figures of the two emigrants are portraits of himself and his wife. One finds, among others, the following references to this work in the artist's diary : ' At the beginning of '53 I worked for about six weeks at the picture of *Last of England,* Emma coming to sit to me, in the most inhuman weather, from Highgate. This work, representing an outdoor scene without sunlight, I painted at it chiefly out of doors, when the snow was lying on the ground. The madder ribbons of the bonnet took me four weeks to paint.'
' Worked at the resumed coat of the Emigrant, from the one I had made on purpose two winters ago, at Hampstead, and have worn since then, it being horrid vulgar.'
3rd January 1855 : ' To work by twelve at the fringe of the shawl—finished it by one. Triumphantly stripped the lay figures, and set the place somewhat to rights, and restored poor Emma her shawl, which she had done without the half of the winter.'
Signed and dated : *F. Madox Brown,* 1855.
Inscribed on frame : *An. Dom.* 1852—*The Last of England.*
Exhibited at the Liverpool Academy in 1856. The picture was retouched in 1859. Smaller versions are in the Tate Gallery and the Fitzwilliam Museum, Cambridge.
Former collections : Bought from the artist by White in 1855 ; B. G. Windus ; T. E. Plint ; Pilgrim ; John Crossley ; C. J. Pooley. Purchased by the Gallery in 1891.
Coll. : *City of Birmingham Art Gallery.*

DYCE, WILLIAM, R.A. (1806–1864)

112. PEGWELL BAY, 1858. Oil on canvas, 24½×34½ inches.

The three figures in the foreground, from right to left, are the artist's wife and her two sisters, Grace and Isabella Brand. The boy with the toy spade is Dyce's son. In the sky is seen the great comet of 1858.

Exhibited at the Royal Academy in 1860, and catalogued as ' Pegwell Bay, Kent, a recollection of October 5, 1858.'

Formerly the property of J. Brand. Purchased by the Gallery in 1894.

Coll. : *The National Gallery, London.*

REID, JAMES (Attributed to)

113. HAMPSTEAD HEATH IN 1859. Oil on canvas, 32½×53½ inches.

Attributed to James Reid, an artist who does not appear to have existed. Possibly by John Ritchie, who exhibited ' Spending a Holiday at Hampstead Heath ' at the British Institution in 1860.

Signed with monogram : *J.R.*, and dated : 1859.

Coll. : *E. Royalton Kisch, Esq., London.*

MILLAIS, SIR JOHN EVERETT, *P.R.A.* (1829–1896)

114. THE BLACK BRUNSWICKER. Oil on canvas, 39×26 inches.

The model for the girl was Mrs. C. E. Perugini, younger daughter of Charles Dickens. The man was a professional model.

Signed with monogram and dated : 1860.

Exhibited at the Royal Academy in 1860.

Former collections : T. E. Plint ; James Price ; James Hall Renton.

Coll. : *The Lady Lever Art Gallery, Port Sunlight.*

MARTINEAU, ROBERT BRAITHWAITE (1826–1869)

115. THE LAST DAY IN THE OLD HOME. Oil on canvas, 41¼×56½ inches.

The inscription on the catalogue, which lies on the floor, reads : ' Catalogue of the valuable contents of Hardham Court, the Seat of Sir Chas. Pulleyne, Bart. Christie & Manson. October 22, 1860. . . .' etc.

Signed and dated : *Robt. B. Martineau*, 1862.

Exhibited at the great Exhibition of 1862.

Presented to the Gallery by E. H. Martineau in 1896.

Coll. : *The Tate Gallery, Millbank, London.*

FRITH, WILLIAM POWELL, R.A. (1819–1909)

116. THE SLEEPING MODEL. Oil on canvas, 25×28 inches.

Painted in 1853. The model was an ' orange-girl of a rare type of rustic beauty ' of whom Frith wanted to do a laughing likeness, but,' he relates, ' after many attempts to rouse an expression that would help me to make a laughing face, I found the worst of hindrances that can afflict a painter come upon me—my model fell fast asleep ; and as nothing that I could say or do would keep her awake, I abandoned the laughing subject and painted " The Sleepy Model," who now sleeps all day long in the Diploma Gallery.' (Cf. W. P. Frith, *My Autobiography*, 1887, vol. I, p. 249.)

Diploma work deposited at the Royal Academy by the artist on his election as an Academician in 1853.

Coll. : *Diploma Gallery, Royal Academy of Arts, London.*

117. RAMSGATE SANDS. Oil on canvas, 60¾×30 inches.

' Ramsgate Sands ' was first conceived in 1851, when Frith was spending the summer at Ramsgate. There he did various drawings from Nature as well as an oil-sketch from which the large picture was painted in London during 1852–53. It was sold to Messrs. Lloyd for £1000 before its exhibition at the Royal Academy in 1854, where it attracted the attention of Queen Victoria. ' She was delighted with " Seaside," ' Frith writes, ' wanted to buy it—found she couldn't, and gave me a commission for a similar subject. . . . Sir C. Eastlake, whose duty it was to attend the Royal party through the entire Exhibition, left them and came to me . . . to enquire into whose possession the " Life at the Seaside "—as it was called in the catalogue— had fallen. " Bought by a picture-dealer," said I, " who for a profit would sell it to her Majesty, or anybody else." Eastlake returned to the Royalties and conveyed my intelligence evidently, for I could see a slight shrug of the Royal shoulders, which said quite plainly, " Picture-dealer ! Outrageous profit, of course." A few days solved the question, for Messrs. Lloyd, hearing of the Queen's desire for the picture, opened up communications through the usual channels, the result being the acquisition of the picture by the Queen for the price Lloyds had paid for it ; their profit accruing from the loan of it for three years for the purpose of engraving.' (Cf. W. P. Frith, *My Autobiography*, 1887, vol. I, pp. 257–258.)

A replica, measuring 30×62 inches, is in the Russell-Cotes Art Gallery, Bournemouth.
Coll. : *His Majesty the King, Buckingham Palace, London.*

118. THE RAILWAY STATION. Oil on canvas, 55½×98¼ inches.

The scene takes place at Paddington Station. The model for the bearded gentleman in the central group was a mysterious Italian nobleman, a refugee from Venice (then under Austrian rule), who thought Frith's daughters Italian. Haydon and Brett, two detectives well known at the time, posed for the officers in mufti arresting a man on the right of the picture.

The painting was commissioned from a preliminary sketch by the picture-dealer L. V. Flatow for the price of £4500 (including the sketch and the copyright). An additional £750 was paid by Flatow to Frith later when the right to exhibit the picture at the Royal Academy, originally reserved by the artist, was rescinded.

Work on ' The Railway Station ' was begun in August 1860. It was completed in March 1862.
Signed and dated : *W. P. Frith, fec*., 1862.

Smaller versions of the picture are in the Leicester Museum and in the collection of C. F. Dendy Marshall, Esq.

Former collections : L. V. Flatow ; M. H. Graves ; Thomas Holloway.
Coll. : *Royal Holloway College, Englefield Green, London.*

119. THE DERBY DAY. Oil on canvas, 39½×87½ inches.

The inspiration for the picture came to Frith during a visit to the Derby of 1856, won by Blink Bonnie. He immediately started to plan the composition and make preliminary studies of separate figures and groups. A small oil-sketch was shown to Jacob Bell, who commissioned the artist ' to paint a picture five or six feet long from it, at the price of fifteen hundred pounds.' Work on this was begun on 9th February 1857. Among the models employed were an acrobat from the Drury Lane pantomime with his little son ; Miss Gilbert—' The Pretty Horse-Breaker,' who posed for the lady in a riding-habit ; Miss H——, an actress, whose figure was eventually erased and repainted from one of Frith's daughters ; the jockey Bundy ; friends of the artist and of Bell and professional models. The painting was finished in 1858 and sent to the Royal Academy, where it caused such a stir that a policeman had to stand by it to keep off the crowds and a rail placed before it for protection (such protective measures had been resorted to only once before at the Royal Academy, when Wilkie's ' The Chelsea Pensioners ' was exhibited in 1822). It was later exhibited in Paris and ' then left this country for its travels abroad, first to the Antipodes, then to America, and among other places to Vienna.' (Cf. W. P. Frith, *My Autobiography*, 1887, vol. I, pp. 271–296.)

Signed and dated 1858.

A replica of the picture is in the Corporation Art Gallery, Manchester, and a sketch, lent by the Victoria and Albert Museum, in Bethnal Green Museum, London.

Bequeathed to the Gallery by Jacob Bell in 1859.
Coll. : *The National Gallery, London.*

DEVERELL, WALTER HOWELL (1827–1854)

120. LADY FEEDING A BIRD. Oil on canvas, 33×22½ inches.

Signed : *W. H. D.*
Purchased out of the Mackerell Fund in 1911.
Coll. : *The Tate Gallery, Millbank, London.*

HUGHES, ARTHUR (1832–1915)

121. THE LONG ENGAGEMENT. Oil on canvas, 41½×20½ inches.

Carved on the tree appears the name 'Amy,' which is the title of the first version of this picture, now also at the Birmingham Art Gallery.

Signed and dated : *A. Hughes*, 1859.

First exhibited at the Royal Academy in 1859 with the following quotation from Chaucer as title :

'For how myght ever sweetnesse hav be known
To hym that never tastyd bitternesse ? '

Presented to the Gallery in 1902 by the executors of Dr. Edwin T. Griffiths.

Coll. : *City of Birmingham Art Gallery.*

122. APRIL LOVE. Oil on canvas, 35×19½ inches (arched top).

Signed and dated : *Arthur Hughes*, 1856.

First exhibited at the Royal Academy in 1856.

Former collections : William Morris, who purchased the picture from the artist ; Henry Boddington ; the Leicester Galleries, from whom it was purchased for the Nation out of the Lewis Fund in 1909.

Coll. : *The Tate Gallery, Millbank, London.*

EGG, AUGUSTUS LEOPOLD, R.A. (1816–1863)

123. PAST AND PRESENT (1). Oil on canvas, 25×30 inches.

Signed and dated : *Augt. Egg*, 1858.

124. PAST AND PRESENT (3). Oil on canvas, 25×30 inches.

Signed and dated : *Augt. Egg*, 1858.

The above belong to a set of three paintings entitled 'Past and Present.' (1) represents a husband discovering his wife's infidelity. In (3) are seen his two daughters five years later, 'a fortnight after his death,' praying for their lost mother. (2), which is not reproduced here, depicts the mother crouching in a corner under the Adelphi Arches by the Thames. The happenings in (2) and (3) occur exactly at the same time, as the artist has indicated by the moon and the little cloud beneath it, which are identical in both pictures.

Presented to the Gallery by Mrs. Alec Martin in 1918.

Coll. : *The Tate Gallery, Millbank, London.*

WALKER, FREDERICK, A.R.A. (1840–1875)

125. SPRING. Water-colour, 24½×19¾ inches.

Signed with monogram : *F. W.*, and dated : 1864.

Exhibited at the Old Water-colour Society in 1864.

Bought from the artist by Mr. (afterwards Sir) William Agnew, who later sold the picture to William Leech and bought it back at Christie's in May 1887 for £2000.

Presented to the Museum by the Executors of Sir William Agnew, Bart.

Coll. : *Victoria and Albert Museum, London.*

LEECH, JOHN (1817–1864)

126. SCARBOROUGH SANDS. Oil on canvas, 13¾×18½ inches.

Coll. : *Sir Alec Martin, London.*

127. SCENE AT SANDBATH. Pencil and water-colour, 24½×35 inches.

The inscription at the bottom of the picture reads : ' The female Blondin outdone ! Grand morning performance on the narrow plank by the darling. . . .'

Signed : *John Leech.*

Coll. : *Sir Alec Martin, London.*

WELLS, HENRY TANWORTH, R.A. (1828–1903)

128. VOLUNTEERS AT THE FIRING-POINT. Oil on canvas, $73\frac{1}{4} \times 114\frac{3}{4}$ inches.

The scene takes place in Wimbledon. The figures in the foreground are portraits and represent Edward Ross, Lt.-Col. Lord Elcho, Lt.-Col. The Hon. W. Colville, Lt.-Col. Halford, Martin R. Smith, Stewart Pixley, Capt. Horatio Ross, Capt. Heaton and Capt. Drake.
Signed and dated : *Henry T. Wells*, 1866.
Exhibited in the same year at the Royal Academy.
Substituted for the artist's original Diploma work in 1882.
Coll. : *The Diploma Gallery, Royal Academy of Arts, London.*

TISSOT, JAMES JACQUES JOSEPH (1836–1902)

129. THE BALL ON SHIPBOARD. Oil on canvas, $32\frac{1}{2} \times 50\frac{1}{2}$ inches.

Signed : *J. J. Tissot.*
Exhibited at the Royal Academy in 1874.
Formerly the property of Mrs. Roland Philipson.
Purchased for the Nation through the Chantrey Bequest in 1937.
Coll. : *The Tate Gallery, Millbank, London.*

130. THE LAST EVENING. Oil on canvas, 28×40 inches.

Signed and dated : *J. J. Tissot*, 1873.
Exhibited at the Royal Academy in 1873.
Bequeathed to the Gallery by Charles Gassiot in 1902.
Coll. : *The Guildhall Art Gallery, London.*

131. 'ENTRE LES DEUX MON CŒUR BALANCE.' Oil on canvas, $14\frac{1}{2} \times 21$ inches.

Signed : *J. J. Tissot.*
Coll. : *The Leicester Galleries, London.*

GREAVES, WALTER (1846–1931)

132. HAMMERSMITH BRIDGE ON BOAT-RACE DAY. Oil on canvas, 36×55 inches.

Painted in 1862.
Signed : *W. Greaves.*
Purchased under the terms of the Chantrey Bequest in 1922.
Coll. : *The Tate Gallery, Millbank, London.*

133. LAWRENCE STREET, CHELSEA. Oil on canvas, $15\frac{3}{4} \times 23\frac{1}{2}$ inches.

Painted about 1880.
Signed : *W. Greaves.*
Coll. : *Mrs. Marchant, London.*

INDEX

(The numerals in italics denote the *figure numbers* of illustrations.)

INDEX